D1477301

Umbrellas & Parasols

Jeremy Farrell

The Costume Accessories Series
General Editor: Dr Aileen Ribeiro

B.T. BATSFORD LTD
LONDON

To my mother and the memory of my father

ISBN 0 7134 4874 1

Typeset by Tek-Art Ltd, Kent
and printed in Great Britain by
Anchor Brendon Ltd
Tiptree, Essex
for the publishers
B.T. Batsford Ltd
4 Fitzhardinge Street
London W1H 0AH

Contents

Acknowledgment

I have received a great deal of help while researching and writing this book and thank for their time and their patience my colleagues in other museums, particularly: Penelope Byrde and Myra Mines at the Museum of Costume, Bath; Emmeline Leary at Birmingham Museum; Alison Carter and Annette Carruthers at Cheltenham Museum; Elizabeth Earle at Derby Museum; Kay Staniland at the Museum of London; Jane Tozer and Sarah Levitt at the Gallery of English Costume, Manchester; Madeleine Ginsburg and Sheila Landi at the Victoria & Albert Museum; and Dr Ilid Anthony at the Welsh Folk Museum. For help with specific enquiries and general queries I must thank Janet Arnold; A.G. MacGregor of the Ashmolean Museum, Oxford; Mr Garrett of T. Fox & Co. Ltd; Mr Hargan of Fox Umbrella Frames Ltd; Mr Harvey of James Smith & Sons Ltd; James Snowden and the staff of Nottinghamshire County Library; and the staffs of the Science Museum Library and the Science Research Library. To all the photographers who coped with the intractable subjects of this book I extend my thanks, particularly to Wendy Barnes who also photographed a wide range of reference material. I am very grateful to Deirdre Slocombe for taking such care over the drawing of parasol parts, and to Dr Aileen Ribeiro, and Belinda Baker and Rachel Wright at Batsford for advice and encouragement. To Dr David Taylor, whose interest in umbrellas has been constantly stimulating and whose extensive knowledge of the decorative arts has been at my disposal at every stage, my gratitude is more than I can adequately express.

List of Illustrations

Introduction

Looking at the combination of plastic, lightweight metal alloys and synthetic materials that make up the modern umbrella, it is difficult to believe that anything so practical, so mechanical, could have a history stretching back centuries. Or that the parasol, now a memory of more leisured days, is even older. Egypt, China and India might all claim the initial inspiration which converted the branch of a tree or a hat on a stick into the first parasol, but it seems certain that the parasol or umbrella – the words have the same linguistic root – was designed first to offer protection from the sun rather than the rain.

From its first appearance the parasol was associated with rank, as it was carried over, rather than by, the person it shaded. Egyptian nobles in about 1200 BC had parasols carried over them, but in Assyria that was the king's prerogative. Elsewhere rank was indicated not so much by size as the number of tiers, the Emperor of China's parasol having four, and the King of Siam's seven or nine. Numbers implied wealth and therefore power. In Ava in Burma the ruler was described as 'King of the White Elephants' and 'Lord of the Twenty-Four Parasols'.

The parasol also had religious associations. Nut, the mother goddess of Ancient Egypt, was sometimes compared to a parasol, her body arching over the whole earth, and in both Egypt and India the parasol was associated with the gods of fertility and harvest, death and rebirth. Similarities occur in the legends surrounding Nut's son Osiris, the Hindu god Vishnu, who in his fifth incarnation brought back the rain-giving umbrella of Varuna from Hell, and the Graeco-Roman god Dionysius/Bacchus, whose birthplace was reputed to be in India.

It was probably in connection with the worship of Dionysius that the parasol came to Greece. It was carried over a statue of the god at festivals and later over other Greek gods and goddesses, including Pallas Athene. Athenian women had parasols held over them at feasts in her honour and at the Thesmophoria, a festival connected with Persephone and signifying rebirth. Through these associations the parasol became an essentially female accessory and the connotations

lingered. In Rome, where the parasol seems to have arrived in the third century BC, it is described by Ovid, Claudian, and others as a feminine toy made of gold, or with jewelled ivory handles and embroidered silk covers. It is possible that the Romans used leather sunshades as umbrellas but the relevant passages in Virgil, Juvenal and Martial could also refer to headgear.

After the fall of the Roman Empire the parasol disappeared from written records but at some stage it began to be employed in the ceremonial surrounding the Pope. A brown-and-white parasol is shown among the regalia given to the Papacy, in the person of Pope Sylvester I, by the Emperor Constantine the Great, in a twelfth-century Roman fresco depicting the now-considered spurious Donation of Constantine by which the Emperor ceded the rule of the Western Empire to the Pope. Between 757 and 767 Pope Paul I gave Pepin the Short of France a jewelled parasol after a dispute over lands in North Germany. In the Utrecht Psalter (AD 970) an angel holds a parasol over King David. (As T.S. Crawford has pointed out, this was later copied by French monks who dressed the figures in contemporary fashions, thus unintentionally misleading historians into believing that the umbrella/parasol was in use in England during the tenth century.) In the twelfth century Pope Alexander III granted the Doge of Venice the right to have a parasol carried over him, a right maintained until the office and the Venetian Republic were abolished by Bonaparte in 1797.

By the fifteenth century the papal badge included the parasol above the crossed keys of St Peter. As such it is still used by the Cardinal Camerlengo as acting head of the Roman Catholic Church during an interregnum in the papacy. In heraldic terms it was called a 'pavilion' (from the Latin *papilionus*), or an *ombrellino*, and was usually shown open, striped in the papal colours of red and gold, with a lance-shaped stick. As the power of the Church weakened in the fifteenth century, high-ranking nobility and ecclesiastical dignitaries used the *ombrellino*, but in different colours, and the way was open for it to become a fashionable accessory. But it was to be many years before the umbrella/parasol was generally adopted, and many more still before it lost the mystique which association with royalty and religion had lent it.

Although the two words 'umbrella' and 'parasol' appear to have been interchangeable in early usage, later and modern definitions restrict 'parasol' to a shade against the sun, and 'umbrella' to protection from the rain. The parasol as a symbol of sunny days became associated with frivolity, while the umbrella, oddly because in its modern incarnation it appeared only recently on the scene, became imbued with all the aura of a religious symbol.

Other writers have dealt exhaustively with the history of the umbrella, and to a lesser extent with the parasol. All the present work can hope to do is to try to put both the umbrella and parasol into a historical and fashionable context, so that the workmanship and variety of what is now rather a humble, utilitarian object may be better appreciated. It is not intended to be a definitive study but an introduction to an interesting subject.

1

Manufacture

FRAMES

The most decorative parts of the umbrella and parasol, the cover and the handle, are dealt with in the following chapters; this chapter is principally concerned with the construction of the frame and cover.

Most umbrellas and parasols have a central stick (called a 'fit-up' in the trade) to which a number of ribs (usually eight) are attached. The ribs support the cover and are themselves supported by stretchers from the centre of their length to the tubular runner which slides up and down the stick. The runner is held in place on the stick, usually but not invariably, by one of two springs, the hand spring near the handle or the top spring (see figs 4 and 76).

The various parts of the early umbrella can be seen quite clearly in one of the plates illustrating the work of *le boursier* (bagmaker) in volume IX of Diderot's *Encyclopédie* (fig. 1). (In France, according to guild regulations at this time, umbrellas were made by those who made cloth and leather bags, purses, 'pudding' caps for babies, and buckskin breeches; no such regulations existed in England.) The model is an advanced one similar to that invented by Marius in about 1709 (see fig. 11). The stick unscrews and folds at *g fig. 2, k* and *l fig. 3*. The ribs fold, too, at *l fig. 1*. The stretchers are short and from *fig. 4* would seem to be in pairs, attached through the whalebone ribs. The runner is very short and is held above the spring. Later runners are longer, with a slot for the spring. The spring is almost identical to those on modern umbrellas.

Diderot's *Encyclopédie* gives very little detail about the actual processes of umbrella manufacture. In the workshop, however, one workman is cutting brass wire for stretchers, and another is sewing together panels of leather using two threads simultaneously in the way that shoes are hand-sewn. Covers could also be made of treated silk taffeta. It seems that whereas the umbrella was always made to fold, the parasol could also be made rigid, the cover being one circular piece of waxed cloth or taffeta supported on cane ribs with a turned stick. This may be a survival from an earlier period. Both types had disadvantages: one could collapse in wind; the other was

difficult to store. It may have been for the rigid parasol that the marquise hinge was invented, to enable the cover to lie flat against the stick.

The *Encyclopédie Méthodique* of 1783 goes into greater detail about construction. Parasol covers could be made of lightweight materials including paper, straw or feathers; umbrella covers from leathers, waxed cloth, taffeta or any flexible fabric. Sticks could be in one piece or made to fold, with stretchers in pairs or single with one forked end. Ribs could be whalebone or, apparently, copper or iron wire. The cover was cut in gores across the fabric and was attached to the ribs in three places along each seam. In addition to these two main types, a parasol-walking-stick had been invented in which the parasol part was contained within a hollow stick, and an automatic-opening umbrella whose metal frame was held closed by a spring which when released opened the umbrella. It seems to have been collapsed by pulling on cords, and could be folded (for even the iron or brass ribs were hinged) to fit into a pocket or a hat-band.

These two French encyclopaedias give some idea of what an eighteenth-century umbrella looked like and how it was made. Nothing similar seems to exist in English, which implies that the British umbrella industry was not as advanced as that of the French. During the first half of the nineteenth century, however, it caught up, but whereas the French industry was famed for expensive, exquisitely finished productions, the English was noted for its cheapness, ascribed chiefly to the importation of duty-free raw materials from British colonies and to cheap labour.

From the Report of the Juries of the Great Exhibition, published in 1852, it is possible to build up an accurate picture of how an umbrella was made before the inventions of Holland and Fox transformed the industry in the 1850s.[1] The frame maker himself needed a capital of only between three and six pounds to set up in business with such basic equipment as a small circular saw, a lathe, drills, a rose cutter for forming tips, a paring knife, a vice, four pairs of pliers and a 'weighing board'. Sticks, ribs, stretchers and runners were supplied ready prepared; the wooden sticks, when crooked, were bent

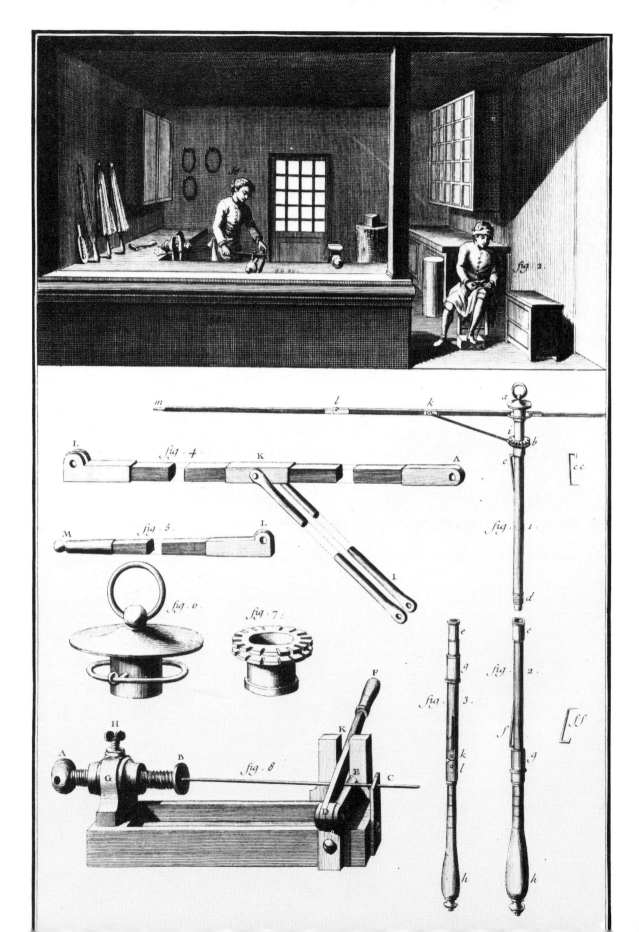

1   One of three plates illustrating the work of le
boursier *(the bagmaker, who also made umbrellas) in*
Diderot's *and* d'Alembert's Encyclopédie, *1763.*

with steam or hot sand by specialist handle makers,
sometimes attached to workshops; the 'furniture' – the
metal parts – came chiefly from Birmingham. The stick
had to be sawn to the correct length, tapered to take the
ferrule, and given two saw-cuts to take the springs, both
of which were bent by hand, and hammered into place;
the lower end through a drilled hole, the top held in
place by a cross wire. Head wires were pushed through
a hole above the top spring to take the ribs. Each rib was
pared and rubbed smooth, given a ball-shaped end and
drilled. Brass strip was wound round it at the opposite
end to the ball and at the centre, and both were drilled to
take wires. The stretchers were attached and the ribs
were 'weighed'; that is, sorted into sets according to
strength. Each set was then 'threadled' at the stretcher
to the runner and then on to the head wires, four per wire.
Altogether the umbrella was reckoned to have passed
135 times through the hands of workmen, and all for the
price of ¾d. to 1d. in the case of umbrellas, 2d. to ¾d. for
parasols. Handmade umbrellas are produced in much
the same way today, the main difference being that the
metal ribs are ready made and are threadled on to a top
notch attached to the stick. Each spring is still made from
wire and attached to the stick in the old way.

In addition to umbrellas constructed on a wooden
stick, there were those made entirely of metal, needing
only a handle and spike to complete them. According to
the Report of the Juries of the Great Exhibition, they were
made for between 7d. and 10d. each, and though more
expensive than those with cane ribs (1d. each) or
whalebone ribs (2½d. each), were much more compact.
Nearly all of them were made in Birmingham using ribs
made there or at Stocksbridge near Sheffield, and
Birmingham-made furniture. They were covered and
finished mainly in London and Manchester.

Although metal ribs had been known in France since
the 1780s, it seems unlikely that they were very popular,
because they were expensive, and also because being
made of iron or brass they were easily bent out of shape.
In 1840 Henry Holland of Birmingham patented (No.
8498) tubular ribs in tempered steel with bits or joints of
brass indented to fit into one end of the ribs, and a brass
rib tip at the other end. These bits or joints were
described as 'equally applicable to umbrellas and
parasols when solid steel or other metal rods or ribs are
used', suggesting that solid steel ribs were already
available. No British patent has been traced for them and
the French patents need much research. The drawings

*2   Advertisement for Samuel Fox & Co.'s solid steel
ribs, 1848; they were later sold under the trade name
'Arcus'.*

accompanying Holland's patent illustrate a middle bit or
git with two flaps below the rib between which the
stretcher was fastened. This was an adaptation of an idea
patented by John Hopper Caney in 1829 (No. 5761). This
git strengthened the umbrella at a point of weakness,
where previously the stretcher had been joined through
the rib itself. Luke Hébert in *The Engineer's and
Mechanic's Encyclopaedia*, first published in 1836,
stresses the importance of Caney's git, and the various
top notches patented by Samuel Hobday in 1821, Francis
Deakin in 1823, and Caney in 1829 (as these are of limited
application, they are dealt with in the 'Umbrellas' section
of Chapter 3), in reducing the cost of the umbrella by
half. Henry Holland invented probably the first
commercially successful steel rib. By 1843 they were
common enough to be mentioned in the *Penny
Cyclopaedia* ('Very light and compact umbrellas are
made with ribs of steel instead of whalebone or cane').
However, Holland's work was to a large extent eclipsed
by Samuel Fox who started to produce a solid steel rib at
his wire-drawing factory at Stocksbridge near Sheffield

in 1847.[2] His ribs had an integral ball-shaped rib tip, a countersunk hole through which the cover ties could be attached, a git that lay flush with the top of the rib, and a flattened end for fixing to a top notch. They were successful and were retained in production by S. Fox & Co. under the trade name 'Arcus' until 1920.[3] As early as 1849 Fox bought tubular sticks, top notches and runners from Thomas Cox of Birmingham and sold complete frames as well as sets of ribs.

In 1850 Henry Holland made his tubular rib elliptical so that one flat side could lie against the cover, rounding one end to take an ivory tip. Ribs were annealed like pen nibs, another Birmingham trade. In 1852, however, Samuel Fox produced what he called 'trough-shaped' stretchers and ribs which were U-shaped in section. He was immediately challenged by Holland who claimed that the new ribs were merely his own cut in half, and by a Frenchman, Duchamp, who had made tubular ribs in France since 1846. Fox, however, proved his case, and a patent (No. 14,055) was granted in 1852. The new ribs sold under the trade name 'Paragon', and needed new furniture (see fig. 3). Fifteen lengths of rib were sold from eleven to 29 inches, 19s. to 32s. per dozen sets; runners sold at 9s. and notches at 6s. 6d. per gross. The new ribs and frames were more expensive but gradually they ousted all others from the market. They were widely copied, especially after the patent expired in 1869.

Samuel Fox tried to protect his patents by including, from 1850, with each set of ribs a disc, printed with a coat-of-arms, a crest of a running fox and 'Samuel Fox & Co., Trade Mark'.[4] This disc was the reinforcement or inside cap which went between the ribs and the cover at the centre of the umbrella. Fox seems to have been the first to use the reinforcement both for identification and advertisement. A similar disc was used for the Paragon frame, 'S. Fox & Co.'s Patent Paragon' being printed on a ring with the coat-of-arms at the bottom. Later variants had no coat-of-arms. Other manufacturers copied the idea. I.A. Boss's disc, illustrated in the 1862 International Exhibition catalogue, had inverted scalloped edges and 'Warranted Best London Made', two anchors and 'Entered at Stationers' Hall'. These discs became common in the late nineteenth century and are often printed with the name and address of the umbrella maker, or sometimes with that of the retailer. However, the disc as a means of identification was not foolproof, as it was often replaced when an umbrella was re-covered. In general they are to be found only on umbrellas. Parasols and sometimes more expensive umbrellas

were marked, if marked at all, on the runner. In rare cases that mark includes the name and address; more often it is just a name (Sangster's, or Lewis & Allenby, for instance) or initials, and sometimes a trade mark. 'B.E. & Co.', and/or a bishop's mitre and 'Mitre Trade Mark', found on parasols of the 1860s and 1870s, seems to refer to Bishop, Ellis & Co. of London.

As far as Samuel Fox was concerned the disc was not entirely satisfactory, as it could be omitted or replaced easily. So from 1865 (patent No. 2348) it was replaced on one of the stretchers by a little metal plaque with the name cast on it. Later this was altered to a piece of paper gummed to a copper plate, and later still to a piece of tin-plate printed with the running fox trade mark, the firm's name and the frame's trade name. Up to 1970 the name on the frame might also be that of the umbrella maker, as opposed to the frame manufacturer. 'Peerless' and 'Longlive', found on two umbrella frames of the 1960s,

3 *Advertisement for Samuel Fox & Co.'s Paragon frames, 1852.*

probably refer to Peerless Umbrellas Ltd, of Manchester, and E. Olive & Co. Ltd, of London.[5] However, most of the names are those of the frames and provide some indication of date.

In 1870 Fox produced the 'Aegis' frame, which was strengthened by smaller U-shaped pieces of metal at the git and top notch joint, so that the umbrella opened to a flatter shape; using a 24½-inch rib it provided as much shelter as a 26-inch frame. (The length of the rib from top notch to rib tip is also the size of the frame.)[6] The Aegis frame was supplied with a strengthened 'Fortis' runner. In the early 1870s Samuel Fox bought the manufacturing rights of the 'Lock-rib' frame from Hill Bros. of Bristol. The Lock-rib had thicker stretchers so that the ribs fitted inside them when closed, making a much thinner umbrella. The reverse of this, the 'Laurus', in which the stretchers fitted inside the ribs, was introduced in 1888 and was popular for men's umbrellas until production of it ceased in 1936. A stronger version, the 'Primus', which had a double U-section rib, was also introduced in 1888. Other frames are rare; the 'Stabilis' of 1879 had double forked rib and stretcher ends, necessitating twice the number of cuts in the top notch and runner; the 'Automaton' had sprung gits so that it closed automatically, needing no hand spring; the 'Optimus' of 1882 had a curled end and neater top notch and runner; and the 'Felix' of 1885 had ribs which secured the cover seams inside them. In 1898 the Lock-rib was made more compact with a smaller git and was called the 'Paragon (D) tube rib'. In 1935 Fox combined a number of different features and improvements in the 'Beaded Edge' rib, (patent No. 420,709), which became the firm's sole production before and after the Second World War.

Other firms patented frame improvements. The best known was the 'Flexus', developed by Fox employees William Hoyland and Joseph Hayward. In 1875 they set up their own company. The Flexus had solid steel ribs, and twice the number of flat spring stretchers attached in pairs at the runner, and midway between the runner and git diverged to join the ribs. In plan the ribs and stretchers form eight petals. The stretchers were under tension when up so that when released the umbrella closed automatically.

Other Fox improvements affected the stick. In 1902 Henry Jeffry and Joseph Moxon patented a steel tube with an internal rib. This replaced the mild-steel tube in 1903; it was temporarily revived in the 'Foxella' frames of the 1930s.

Although the bent-wire spring is still the most usual form of holding the umbrella open or closed, there were variants from the late 1830s onwards. In 1839 the French manufacturer Cazal invented a long spring with a hook at each end; these caught on to rings on the stick and were released by pressing the spring in the middle. A similar spring was patented by I.A. Boss in 1845, together with a long runner with two pivoted levers, one at each end to hook over rings on the stick. Cazal also used a sprung lever, one end of which was bent and fitted into a hole in the stick. This is the one most commonly found on Cazal's parasols. R. Harrington patented a similar catch, but reversed, in 1862. Other alternatives to the wire spring do not seem to have been successful, except for the flat metal spring commonly found on metal sticks.

COVERS

The cover department is separate from the frame-making department, though often housed in the same building. Whether the frame has been made in the workshop or has come complete on a metal stick from the factory, it is covered in the same way as it has been since the mid-nineteenth century.

The covering material is folded so that all the gores are cut in one operation. The shape is chalked on to the fabric using a wooden template, first on one selvedge and then on the other (umbrella material is specially woven) so that there is minimum waste, and cut out with a sharp knife. The gores are triangular with the equal sides being more or less curved, depending on the number of gores; the larger the number the straighter the sides. Gores in complicated patterns such as checks are cut out individually. The gores are stitched together in pairs, in four, and so on, until the cover is completed. The edge, when not a selvedge, is stitched, and, after 'prevents' or 'preventers' have been attached over the gits to minimize wear at those points, the cover is sewn to the frame by 'tipping', two or three tie stitches attaching each seam to each rib and rib tip. Rosettes of gathered doubled fabric are sewn tightly round the stretchers on the runner and the ribs at the top notch to hide the joints. About 300 hand stitches go into a modern handmade umbrella cover. There would have been more up to the middle of the nineteenth century, as seams and edges were hand stitched by 'tweedling' – running the seam without taking the needle out of the fabric. Machine stitching seems to have come into use in the 1860s, as sewing machines in general came to be more widely adopted.[7] Central reinforcements printed with 'Warranted Best Machine Made' or 'Superior Machine Made' are found in conjunction with lockstitching inside many of the plainer parasols of the 1860s. Once the novelty had worn off, makers of better-quality umbrellas and parasols continued to stitch covers by hand.[8] Brigg and Son were perhaps one of the last to do so and only changed to the sewing machine when they could no longer get women to hand-sew the covers, probably after the Second World War. Brigg umbrellas always

4(**a**)   *Spring patented in France by M. Cazal in 1839; a similar spring was patented in England by I.A. Boss in 1845. The hooks are released from rings on the metal stick by pressing the sprung steel strip between them.*

4(**c**)   *Spring marked 'Harrington Patent' which can be linked to R. Harrington's patent 2347 of 1862, found on parasols.*

4(**d**)   *Rib tip cup, spring loaded, French, marked 'Bte Depose M. & C. Cie'; on a black silk-twill-covered umbrella with a Fox Paragon frame.*

4(**b**)   *Spring found on most Cazal parasols. The runner is stamped 'Cazal, Boulevard des Italiens, Paris'.*

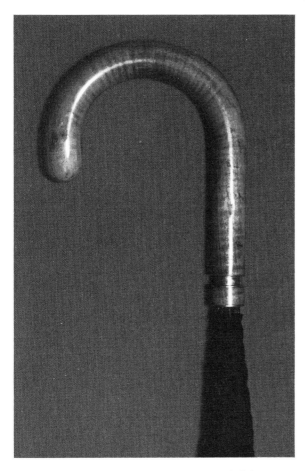

4(e)   Tip cup marked '"Corona" Pat. 364916–31'; on a malacca umbrella handle banded with gold.

4(f)   Parasol joint, patented by J. & H. Tracy, 3230 of 1869, on a brown-painted stick with a brown taffeta cover. The bone ring is marked 'Patent'.

have stitched edges to the covers instead of selvedges.

From the mid-nineteenth century, and, one suspects, before, although there is little information about the industry then, covers were made both in the workshops and by outworkers; in all cases by women, although the cutters were men. In the 1880s parasols in the latest fashion were made in the warehouse; the rest sent out. For the latter, prices might range from 1s.3d. or 1s.6d. each to 9d. per dozen, on which two people worked for two and a half hours. The most the cover maker and her finisher could hope to earn in the busy season, which lasted six or seven weeks, was £1 and 12s., respectively, per week. Finishers and trimmers in the warehouse were paid 10s. and 18s. per week, or from 18s. to 20s. as piece workers.[9] The same system of in- and out-of-shop work continues today for handmade umbrellas.

One of the finishing processes was the stitching-on of the band, a strip of silk matching the cover with a ring at one end to slip over a button and enable the umbrella to be tightly rolled. From the 1840s, after the process of vulcanizing rubber had been discovered, many umbrellas and plain parasols had bands of narrow strips of rubberized material, sometimes no more than one-eighth of an inch wide. The two continue into the present, the button itself being metal, glass or plastic, and sometimes, though rarely, marked with the manufacturer's name. In more modern times it has often been replaced by the press-stud. From the early 1860s the band was often used in conjunction with the rib-tip cup, invented to hold the rib tips closer to the stick so that the cover could be rolled more tightly. Although the first seems to have been a bayonet fitting patented in 1862 by J. Critchley, tip cups did not come into general use until the 1870s. 'Sliding cups to fit over the ends of the ribs and hold the umbrella closed, have been invented, but until recently do not seem to have come much into use.'[10] The earlier ones seem to have been rather clumsy with ogee-shaped sides, probably because until Samuel Fox produced the curved rib in 1873 rib tips did not lie close to the stick. Some cups screwed into place; others were made entirely of rubber and rolled down over the tips. The simple metal band on a bayonet fitting, which was certainly in use in the 1890s, is still made today, but more refined models are also available. T. Fox & Co. still make the 'Regal', a long tip cup, the top of which is hidden behind a metal band so that when lowered no thinness is apparent in the handle; the 'Prince', which has an individually shaped metal former to keep the band in place; and the 'Corona' (patent No. 364,916 of 1931). The latter involves the careful removal of a ring of wood from the end of the handle without cutting through the handle itself, and mounting it between gold bands. These three can only be used when the handle is made separately from the stick. When the handle and stick are all in one the same result may be achieved by a rubber ring. J. Bradbury patented rib tips in 1910 which were made by S. Fox & Co. with a curve to accommodate such a ring. Old rings have mostly perished.[11] Black rubber rings can be found on men's modern umbrellas.

There were other methods of keeping parasols closed. The earliest, which may also have been used on umbrellas, was a ring of metal or ivory attached by a cord or tape to the top-notch end of the cover. It was in use in the nineteenth century up to about 1840 and from 1879 through the 1880s. During the era of the small parasol the most usual method of closure is a tasselled cord with a bell-shaped bead of ivory or bone at one end which slots into a brass plate. This type of fastening is usually attached midway along the cover rather than at the edge. From the 1890s onwards the parasol borrows the band from the umbrella or uses a double cord around the rib tips to fasten over a button.

Once the band had been attached the umbrella was returned to the workshops to be fitted with a ferrule at the end of the stick and a metal open cap over the top of the cover. Later parasols often had a ruched band instead of the cap. After washing (in the case of umbrellas) and ironing, the umbrella/parasol would be ready to be sold.

In the late eighteenth and early nineteenth centuries many manufacturers had only a small workforce making umbrellas for retail, repairing and re-covering. Umbrellas of this period, it seems, were prone to accidents. '"I beg your pardon, sir", said a little prim, wheezing old gentleman, . . . "but have you ever observed, when you have been in an omnibus on a wet day, that four people out of five always come in with large cotton umbrellas, without a handle at the top, or the brass

SAMUEL FOX & COMPANY, LIMD.

OLD STYLE   NEW STYLE

NEW RING TIP

It will be observed that the **new patent tip** is so shaped that when the several ribs close around the stick **a groove is thereby formed** in which the Indiarubber Ring rests securely and holds the Ribs firmly in position—Fig. 3. *This does away with the continual adjustment of the ring necessary in the old style.*

The improved Tip has quite a neat appearance even if the Ring is omitted.

OTHER ADVANTAGES. In the **new tip** the loop wire does not protrude at all and this allows the Ribs to lie closer to the stick than at present. Also, in consequence of the loop being set back, the sticks of new umbrellas in stock do not so easily get marked by the friction in opening to show to customers.

*Stocksbridge Works,
Near Sheffield,
June, 1910.*

5   *Samuel Fox & Co.'s new rib tip of 1910, patented by John Bradbury (patent No. 6259).*

spike at the bottom?"[12] Some umbrella makers were associated with other trades of a similar nature. Michael Lawrence, Umbrella Maker, of Bull Street, Birmingham, in 1785, also made walking sticks and fishing rods. T. Power, Umbrella, Parasol and Furniture Manufacturer, in the same street, in 1821, also sold table mats, doylies, bathing caps and hat covers. T. Painter, Umbrella and Parasol Maker of Piccadilly, London, who supplied Queen Victoria and her mother, the Duchess of Kent, with parasols in the 1850s, also made fishing rods and tackle. Once umbrellas became fashionable for men they were made and sold in conjunction with establishments for men – tobacconists, for instance, or hairdressers; both James Smith & Co., founded in 1830 and established in New Oxford Street in 1867, and T. Fox & Co., established in 1868, had hairdressing departments.

Parasols were sold by umbrella makers and in fancy-goods warehouses. They were stocked by linen drapers. One which sold 'every description of goods fifty per cent under cost price', in *Sketches by Boz* by Charles Dickens (1836-7), had green parasols at 2s.9d. each, French kid shoes at the same price, and 350,000 boas from 1s.11½d. each. Later in the century, as general drapers expanded into departmental stores, parasols were sold either in a department of their own or in the fur department, so that each might cover the other in their slack seasons.[13] All departmental stores, to judge from their catalogues, offered a re-covering service, and this seems to have been done on a scale difficult to contemplate nowadays. In 1895 the *Woman at Home* magazine recommended setting aside 7s. out of a £10-a-

6(a)   Automatic opener: yellow-painted double stretchers and stick, mid-nineteenth century.

6(b)   Telescopic umbrella with two sets of stretchers and half ribs, telescopic stick, printed nylon cover, c. 1980.

year dress allowance for an umbrella or re-covering the same. The *Girl's Own Paper* in 1889 suggested that for a man earning £1 per week, 9s. out of £8 9s. per year for dress should be paid for an umbrella to last two years. Cheap umbrellas could be bought in shops, but there was also a roaring trade in second-hand umbrellas collected by men shouting 'Umbrellas to mend' or 'Any old umbrellas to sell?' and sold refurbished at street corners or on market stalls.[14]

PATENTS AND REGISTERED DESIGNS

Perhaps more than any other costume accessory, the umbrella has attracted the inventor. The first patent connected with the umbrella, for 'a machine for supporting an umbrella which may be fixed to any saddle or wheeled carriage' was granted to Mark Bull in 1780, and the first for an actual umbrella to John Beale in 1786. Up to 1840 there were only 22 patents covering umbrellas, parasols and walking sticks, but from then on the number grows considerably; 78 between 1855 and 1860, 155 between 1870 and 1875, and an average of 43 a year between 1895 and 1904. Each part of the umbrella and parasol was more than once the object of improvement and innovation, sometimes in very similar terms. Among the enduring ideas was the cranked stick which enabled the open umbrella to be centred over the head, instead of to one side. It appears in Beale's patent of 1786 and thereafter with regularity. Another was the cycloidal umbrella with the stick placed off-centre; once, in 1888, to form the stalk of a leaf-shaped cover. The walking-stick umbrella appears in various forms; chiefly with a detachable cover and frame which could be housed in the hollow stick, or as an umbrella inside a telescopic case which could be carried in the pocket. One of the first versions of the latter was the 'ad libitum umbrella or parasol' patented by Phillis Brown Thompson in 1809. Telescopic and automatic-opening umbrellas appear frequently in all sorts of forms, with folding or telescopic ribs, half ribs, or with two or more sets of stretchers.

Some of the patents were imaginative rather than practical, and many can never have been made except perhaps in prototype. So many of them are irrelevant to the study of the umbrella and parasol as costume accessories that they have been referred to here only if they can be linked to an existing model or can provide a means of dating similar examples. In trying to locate a particular patent it is worth noting that until 1915 each year has its own series of patents, and that thereafter they run consecutively.

Although patents are relatively easy to track down, registered designs are not. Fortunately, in the early years after 1842 manufacturers were sufficiently proud of

7 Unusual shapes:
(**a**) adapted pagoda shape with the curve of the twelve ribs flattened near the tips, marked 'Pat. No. 14388' on frame; this can be linked to J. Rose's patent of 1910. Green silk cover.

(**b**) Ten Paragon ribs, half of which turn up and the other half down. Although unmarked, it is probably connected with J. Rose's patent 22,961 of 1912 in which one or more ribs were bent up 'so as to allow the escape of air in a storm'.

their designs to put the whole date of registration on the runner, but they do not seem to have used the diamond registration mark from 1843 to 1884. The consecutive numbering system with the prefix 'Rd. No.', which replaced the diamond mark, was used, however, and sometimes numbers can be linked to a date and/or manufacturer. However, the designs are not always found where one would expect them to be. The handle, marked 'Reg. No. 173511', on a parasol in the Museum of Costume and Textiles, Nottingham (colour plate 6) has been traced to Henry Howell & Co., Cane and Stick Manufacturers, 180 Old Street, London, and was registered on 26 July 1891, but was found in Class 3, which, according to pre-1884 registration, would be glass![15] The upward-curving ribs can be traced to J. Allcock's patent No. 20, 454 of 1894. To have both handle and frame covered by registered design and patent is very rare.

In general patents gave protection for fifteen years, registered designs for two or three.

2

1600-1750

Until the middle of the eighteenth century the words 'parasol' and 'umbrella' are practically synonymous. In Nicholas Bailey's *Etymological English Dictionary, being also an Interpreter of Hard Words* of 1721, a parasol is 'a sort of Small Canopy or Umbrello to keep off the Rain' and an 'Umbrello', 'a sort of skreen that is held over the Head for preserving from the sun or rain; also a wooden frame cover'd with cloth or Stuff to keep of [*sic*] the sun from a window'. Both words descend from Latin roots, and have much the same meaning, the parasol, however, including a reference to the sun (*solus*); the umbrella just to shade (*umbella*). Whether the parasols and umbrellas mentioned in documents offered protection from the sun or rain can be deduced only from the context, but, as can be seen from the above definition of 'umbrello', the words could mean much more than the collapsible article with which we are familiar, and should be treated with caution. To add to the confusion in what seems to be its first appearance in the British Isles, the parasol is defined by neither word. In an inventory compiled for Mary, Queen of Scots and dated 25 November 1561, is listed among the canopies and cloths of state 'Item ane litle cannabie of crammosie satine of thre quarter lang furnisit with freingeis and tassis maid of gold and crammosie silk/mony litle paintit buttonis all serving to mak Schaddow afoir the Quene.'[1] This, whether it was a square canopy like a cloth of state or a round one similar to a modern umbrella, was obviously portable and intended to offer protection against the sun. If the 'quarter' referred to is a quarter of a yard, this canopy would be 27 inches long, a reasonable length for a parasol. The buttons presumably were decorative.

In 1565 Mary's valet de chambre, Servais de Condez, who was responsible for much of her movable property, compiled a list of all items issued by him to other people. In July he writes, 'Plus a la Rayne ung petit pavillon qui sert donbre devan sa Majestez lequel est à son cabinet.'[2] Although this could refer to a small tent it is more likely to refer to a parasol, for not only is it issued to the Queen herself; it is described in similar terms to the papal *papilionus* or *ombrellino*, and was obviously small

enough, and perhaps ornate enough, to be kept in the Queen's private apartments ('cabinet' at this date is more likely to be a room than a cupboard). Later, presumably when it is no longer needed, it is returned to be stored with the furniture, and a note is made to that effect. No detail is given of its construction or history, but it is likely to have been after the Italian model and brought from France by Mary when she returned to Scotland in 1561 as the widow of Francis II. It is quite possible that his mother, Catherine de' Medici, introduced the parasol to France from Italy. Previous writers have found no mention of parasols in her inventories, but it is possible that they are there, disguised as canopies or pavilions. In the Musée de l'Hôtel de Cluny in Paris there was in the nineteenth century the remains of an ivory parasol reputed to have belonged to Diane de Poitiers, mistress of Catherine de' Medici's husband, Henry II. From a mid-nineteenth century engraving[3] it can be seen that the parasol has six ribs, rectangular in section, fitted at one end to a top notch, and at the middle to stretchers, which in turn fit into a notched ring sliding on a stick to open and fold the parasol in the usual way. Although the traditional attribution to Diane de Poitiers might be doubted, it seems from the slender evidence we have that it could be a parasol frame of the mid-sixteenth century.

Elizabeth I, too, probably had a parasol. A canopy of crimson damask with a mother-of-pearl handle is listed in an inventory of her possessions in 1600.[4] But even in France they were something of a rarity. In *Dialogues of the new French language Italianised* by Henri Estienne, 1578, two gentlemen discuss the parasol:

CELTOPHILE . . . and à propos of pavilion, have you ever seen what some of the lords in Spain or Italy carry or cause to be carried about in the country to defend themselves, not so much from the flies, as from the sun? It is supported by a stick, and so made that being folded up and occupying very little space, it can when necessary be opened immediately and stretched out in a circle so as to cover three or four persons.

His friend remarks that though he has never seen one he

has often heard them described; ladies, he feels, would regard men carrying them as effeminate.[5]

The first representation of a parasol in Britain, apart from that in the Utrecht Psalter noted above, is probably in the portrait of Sir Henry Unton. This strange picture has vignettes of important events in his life, including his birth, marriage and death, surrounding the main portrait like a strip cartoon. In one of these vignettes he is depicted on horseback carrying a white parasol on his travels through Italy between 1575 and 1580 (fig. 8). As the portrait was commissioned by his widow, shortly after his death in 1596, the parasol must either have been familiar to the unknown artist or copied from one Sir Henry brought back from his travels. The parasol at this date was still sufficiently rare to warrant a fairly lengthy entry in Florio's dictionary *A Worlde of Wordes* (1598). There the Italian word *Ombrella* is defined as 'a fan, a canopie, also a testoon or cloth of state for a prince; also a kind of round fan or shadowing that they use to ride with in summer in Italy; a little shade'.[6] Thomas Coryat in his *Crudities*, published in 1611, goes into even more detail, describing a parasol he had seen in Italy in 1608:

8 *Sir Henry Unton riding through Italy. A detail of a posthumous portrait painted c. 1596, artist unknown. The parasol is white.*

Many of them (Italians) do carry other fine things of a far greater price, that will cost at least a ducat which they commonly call in the Italian tongue Umbrellaes, that is, things that minister shadow onto them for shelter against the scorching heat of the sun. These are made of leather, something answerable to the form of a little canopy, and hooped in the inside with divers little wooden hoops that extend the umbrella in a pretty large compass.

He adds that they were chiefly used by horsemen who fasten one end of the stick against their thighs.[7]

From the description these parasols would seem to have been bell-shaped and held out by concentric hoops, rather than the inverted saucer-shape held out on ribs. Coryat adds that though the umbrella would be familiar to those who had travelled in Italy, to others it would be a novelty.

The parasol was familiar enough to a cultured audience to be mentioned, usually metaphorically, by a number of writers from the early seventeenth century onwards. Ben Jonson in *The Devil is an Ass* describes a woman who had tripped over, as 'flat-spread as an umbrella'.[8] Michael Drayton in a poem in 1630 sent to his mistress some turtle-doves which 'like Umbrellas, with their feathers/Shield you in all sorts of weathers'.[9] Unfortunately the umbrella is often familiar enough to warrant no further description.

Parasols also appear in paintings. In 1623 Van Dyck depicted the Marchesa Elena Grimaldi under a crimson silk parasol borne by a negro page (fig. 9). Although her portrait might have provided the prototype for such portraits as those of Anne, Duchess of Bedford and Lady Mary Wortley Montagu, both painted in the 1730s and representing the sitters under parasols borne by negro pages, the more immediate origin for this image probably lies in the figure of a woman in oriental dress under a parasol carried by a slave, which was almost a commonplace in advertisements for tea, coffee and eastern goods. It even finds its way into embroidery; the Queen of Sheba is so depicted in an embroidered picture of *c.* 1650 in the Victoria & Albert Museum.

The East India Company was granted a royal charter in 1600 for the collection of spices from India and the Far East but it was not until after 1660 that other oriental wares began to arrive in quantity to be bought up by the luxury-loving society which existed in France after Louis XIV reached his majority in 1656 and in England after the Restoration of Charles II in 1660. In 1664 John Evelyn describes a cargo sent on an East India Company ship by Jesuits in China and Japan to Paris.[10] He list rhinoceros horns; vests (presumably mandarins' robes) embroidered in gold and silver ('as for splendour and vividness we have nothing in Europe approaches'); sharp knives; fans 'like those our ladys use but much larger, and with long handles curiously carved, and filled with Chinese characters'; high quality paper; prints; 'pictures of men and Countries, rarely painted on a sort of gumm'd *Calico* transparent as glasse'; fabric flowers, beasts and birds; and drugs. In the same year the title page of his book *Kalendarium Hortense* depicted a negro page carrying a parasol. This coincidence has led some writers to believe that the fans mentioned by Evelyn were really parasols; in fact the parasol was already known to him, for in 1644 during his travels in France and Italy he and his party bought 'Umbrellos against the heate',[11] and he would surely have referred to anything of that sort as an 'umbrello'.

The appearance of the parasol for much of the century can be deduced only from pictures, as no complete parasol from this period seems to have survived. Nearly all seem to have had a stick of turned wood with the ribs of rectangular-section laths of wood which opened out to give the parasol a flat appearance. The stretchers attached to one side of the ribs would also have been wooden laths, and the runner held up by a pin through the stick. Such a pin is seen in the engraving of the parasol frame belonging to Diane de Poitiers, and on a nineteenth-century Persian parasol in the Museum of London. The cover of the latter is crimson silk embroidered with gold, and the pin may have been a more practical means of supporting the weight of the cover than a spring. The covers of the seventeenth century were of silk or leather and richly painted or embroidered. According to an inventory of 1637, Louis XIII of France had no less than eleven sunshades of taffeta in different colours,[12] but he was noted for his effeminacy.

A parasol cover of the late seventeenth to early eighteenth century in the Museum of London is of cream silk embroidered with coloured silks and gold, and has a scalloped edge which would fall over the ends of the ribs (colour plate 1). This was presumably intended for the type of parasol which opened in the manner of a Japanese sunshade, and this was the form that was to continue until at least 1773, for in an engraving of that year Jean Michel Moreau the Younger depicts one which, with its flat, fringed cover and elaborately turned handle, is indistinguishable from a parasol of the seventeenth century.

In the last quarter of the seventeenth century, an alternative shape, the shallow cone, became popular. This can be seen in an engraving of 1676, *A Lady Walking in the Countryside*, by J-D. de St Jean after N. Bonnart (fig. 10). Such a shape could not have been supported on inflexible wooden ribs. Antoine

9   *Marchesa Elena Grimaldi, wife of Marchese Nicola Cattaneo, 1623, by Sir Anthony van Dyck. The parasol has a crimson silk cover with fringe or braid at the scalloped edges and on the top surface. The stretchers, probably ten in number, lie very close to the ribs.*

Furetière's *Dictionnaire*, published in the late seventeenth century, describes the parasol as:

> a small portable piece of furniture, or round covering, carried in the hand, to defend the head from the great heat of the sun; it is made of a circle of leather, taffety, of oilcloth &c. It is suspended to the end of a stick; it is folded or extended by means of some ribs of whalebone which sustain it. It serves also to defend one from rain, and then it is called by some parapluie umbrella.[13]

Whalebone would also have made the parasol light enough to be carried by the person it was protecting, somewhere between the 3lb 8oz of a parasol of 1645 and the 1lb 13oz of a parasol of *c.*1740.[14]

10   Lady Walking in the Countryside, *engraved by J-D. de St Jean, c. 1670. The lady is fashionably dressed and carries a parasol with a turned wood or ivory handle and a fringed silk cover; either the stretchers are very short, or the parasol is rigid. Fashion plates, of which this is one of the earliest, helped to disseminate French fashions.*

A painting of the gardens at Versailles by Jean Baptiste Martin the Elder, probably dating from the 1690s, shows three flat parasols and one very shallow and conical. Two of the flat parasols, in red, are attached to the back of a little carriage which has two seats one behind the other and looks as if it might have been pulled by servants. The other flat one is yellow, with a hanging scalloped edge, and what appears to be an ivory knob at the ferrule end. The conical example, also red, is carried by a footman. In the foreground a negro page carries his mistress's train and a closed red parasol.

By the middle of the seventeenth century some parasols had reached Britain. In his will of 1618 Robert Toft mentions 'an umbrello of perfumed leather with a gold fringe about it, which I brought out of Italy'.[15] In the catalogue, published in 1656, of the Tradescant Collection, then at Lambeth, appears among the utensils

'an umbrello'. This was part of the collection subsequently acquired by Elias Ashmole and is mentioned in a catalogue of 1685 as 'No. 423 umbrella indica' – Indian umbrella; *indica* in this context could merely mean foreign or might indicate an oriental origin, possibly China. The umbrella itself, unfortunately, is no longer part of the Tradescant Collection preserved in the Ashmolean Museum, Oxford. For at least the first three-quarters of the seventeenth century the parasol was a rarity in Britain, mentioned perhaps by travellers, brought home as a souvenir by one or two, but not used in any practical sense in this country.

For the last quarter of the seventeenth century references to parasols in English are still sparse. In February 1676 John Locke, while travelling in Southern France, notes in Montpellier, 'A pretty sort of cover for women rideing in the sun, made of straw, something of the fashion of tin covers for dishes.'[16] This would be taken as a description of a type of hat were it not for his note in the margin, 'Parasols'. John Lough, editor of Locke's journals of his travels, states that the word 'parasol' was originally used for headgear, but this entry could be interpreted either way.

Catherine of Braganza is said to have brought parasols in her trousseau when she married Charles II in 1662. This is quite possible, for the Portuguese, who were as ardent travellers as the Spanish from the fifteenth century onwards, had a colony at Goa on the west coast of India from which they imported oriental goods. In a book of travels in 1598 Johann Theodor and Johann Israel de Bry depicted Portuguese merchants in India walking under long-handled parasols of an inverted saucer shape. One is shown folded.[17]

Although she brought with her 'Indian Cabinets and large trunks of laccar as had never before been seen here',[18] Catherine's clothes, particularly what Evelyn described as 'monstrous fardingals or Guard Infantas' were regarded with disfavour at the English court, and Catherine herself soon abandoned them. Neither her parasols, if she had any, nor the parasols carried over the ambassador from the King of Bantam – his credentials and his presents, when he had audience with Charles II in May 1682 – started any kind of fashion.[19] The King of Bantam's parasols were subsequently presented to Prince Rupert. They were probably kept simply as curiosities; indeed 'umbrellows' were defined as such in a sale at the Blue Coat Coffee House, St Swithin's Lane, London in 1687.[20] Neither of the two great diarists of the period – John Evelyn, who covered the period from 1620 to 1705, nor Samuel Pepys, writing between 1660 and 1669 – mentioned the parasol as a fashionable accessory, and both commented on contemporary fashions. More tellingly, neither the parasol nor the umbrella is mentioned in *Mundus Muliebris*, a detailed list of dress and toilet items compiled by Mary Evelyn and her father and published in 1690. The parasol does not seem to have been at all fashionable until the 1730s when it appeared in two portraits. The first, at Woburn Abbey, shows Anne, Duchess of Bedford between 1725 and 1733. She wears a turban and a knee-length jacket of velvet trimmed with fur over a silk skirt; on her right stands a negro page holding a long-handled, conical parasol. The other painting shows Lady Mary Wortley Montagu, the renowned traveller and letter writer, also in oriental dress with a negro page and parasol. In both the parasol is carried as a fashionable accessory, but the fashion is probably that of fancy dress rather than everyday costume. Almost contemporary with these paintings is the portrait of the Duchess of Queensberry as a milkmaid. Although it is possible that the parasol was used in England in the late seventeenth century and in the first half of the eighteenth century, there appears as yet no evidence for it, and indeed Dutch influence and wars with France might have acted against the adoption of a French fashion which was, in any case, confined to a few.

UMBRELLAS

The umbrella, which protects against the rain, rather than the sun, has always been the poor relation of the frivolous, expensive parasol. Consequently, if references to the parasol are few, those to umbrellas are even more sparse. In addition, the date of their arrival in Britain is open to speculation.

In the inventories of Louis XIII for 1637, three umbrellas of oiled cloth, trimmed on the underside with gold and silver lace, were listed together with eleven coloured taffeta parasols.[21] Oilcloth had been invented by Giacomo Marigi of Turin[22] but the formula, closely guarded at first, soon became common knowledge. Depending on the quality of the umbrella, the fabrics treated could be silk, linen or cotton. Other waterproofing agents were varnish or melted wax, both of which tended to crack in use.

Antoine Furetière in his *Dictionnaire*, published in the late seventeenth century in France, referred to umbrellas by the modern · name of *parapluie* (confusingly, in France *une ombrelle* is a parasol, usually more expensive and lavishly trimmed than *le parasol*, which is a sunshade), and presumably by that time they were reasonably common.

Like the parasol, the umbrella crept unannounced into English life. What appears to be an umbrella is carried behind a lady in a view of the King's Bath, Bath, in 1662, by W. Schellinks. Bath was both hilly and wet and people of fashion seem to have used the umbrella first there. In *A Tale of a Tub* (1696) by Jonathan Swift, Jack, representing Protestant Dissenters, was described as wearing 'a large skin of parchment [which] served him for a night cap when he went to bed, and for an umbrella in rainy weather'.[23] Ten or so years later there was a spate of references to umbrellas in the newspapers. In the famous case of the petticoat in number 116 of the *Tatler*, 1709, a machine is constructed 'of several legs, that could contract or open itself like the top of an umbrella' so that the newly invented hooped petticoat could be examined in court by Isaac Bickerstaff, Esquire, Censor of Great Britain. In number 238 of the *Tatler*, 'Mr Humphrey Wagstaff' (Jonathan Swift) described the effects of a city shower:

> To shops in crowds the daggled females fly,
> Pretend to cheapen goods, but nothing buy.
> The Templar spruce, while ev'ry spout's abroach,
> Stays till 'tis fair, yet seems to call a coach.
> The tuck'd sempstress walks with hasty strides,
> While streams run down her oil'd umbrella's sides.

Swift also painted in graphic detail what the pedestrian had to encounter in the way of rubbish washed down the gutters. Obviously those that could afford it used sedan chairs, or coaches, as the lawyer mentioned above pretends to do. The umbrella was used only by those who had to go on foot, and even then, chiefly by women. The *Female Tatler* for 12 December 1709 had a notice:

> The young gentleman belonging to the Custom House, that for fear of the rain borrowed the umbrella at Will's Coffee House, in Cornhill, of the mistress, is hereby advertised that to be dry from head to foot on the like occasion, he shall be welcome to the maid's pattens.[24]

Borrowed and unreturned umbrellas are not a new phenomenon! In 1708, in the play *The Fine Lady's Airs* by Thomas Baker, Mrs Trapes of Leadenhall Street was described as 'hauling away the umbrellas for the walking gentry'.[25] She was probably a pickpocket. A Mrs Trapes also appeared in John Gay's *The Beggar's Opera* (1728).

John Gay had referred to the umbrella as a female accessory in a poem in his *Trivia* in 1712:

> Good housewives all the winter's rage despise,
> Defended by the riding-hood's disguise,
> Or, underneath th' umbrella's oily shed
> Safe thro' the wet on clinking pattens tread.
> Let Persian dames th' umbrella's ribs display,
> To guard their beauties from the sunny ray,

Or sweating slaves support the shady load,
When Eastern monarchs show their state abroad.
Britain in winter only shows its aid
To guard from chilly showers the walking maid.

He seems by this to confirm that the parasol was not carried in Britain at this date, and that, because of the climate, the umbrella preceded the parasol into general use. The only men who could use the umbrella with impunity were doctors and clergymen whose professional duties took them out in the rain. The purchase of an unbrella is mentioned in the accounts of several churches, probably for holding over the officiating clergyman at rainswept funerals. St Nicholas's Church, Newcastle upon Tyne, paid 25s. for one in 1717, and St John the Baptist's Church, Chester, 10s. for another in 1727;[26] 15s. for an umbrella appears in the household accounts for 1727 of the Earl of Thanet.[27]

The most famous man to carry an umbrella at this period was a fictional one. In *Robinson Crusoe*, published in 1719, Daniel Defoe described his hero making an umbrella like those he had seen in Brazil where they were carried against the heat.

At last I made one that answer'd indifferently well. The main difficulty I found was to make it let down. I could make it to spread, but if it did not let down, too, and draw in, it was not portable for me any way but just over my head which wou'd not do. However, at last, as I said, I made one to answer, and covered it with skins, the hair upwards, so that it cast off the rains like a penthouse, and kept off the sun so effectually, that I could walk out in the hottest of the weather with greater advantage than I could before in the coldest, and when I had no need of it, cou'd close it and carry it under my arm.

Crusoe had, incidentally, invented the first *en-tout-cas*, but even he did not set a male fashion.

Fashionable umbrellas of this period seem not to have survived. One church umbrella at Cartmel Priory in Lancashire appears, from the photograph in T.S. Crawford's *A History of the Umbrella*, to be of seventeenth- or early eighteenth-century construction. The ribs and stretchers are wooden laths and the stick, handle and runner turned wood. Umbrellas constructed like this would have been heavy, as well as large. From that day to this, weight and compactness have been two of the obsessions of the umbrella manufacturer. To solve these problems one French umbrella maker, M. Marius,

invented a collapsible umbrella. In 1715 he published an advertisement showing a woman with an ornate parasol, and a man with a *parapluye*; from hooks nearby hang bags to hold the parasol and the umbrella when folded. To concentrate his invention into a compass small enough to fit into a pocket Marius probably used a hollow stick, perhaps telescopic or in sections screwing together, and whalebone ribs, probably hinged. Unfortunately none of his umbrellas have survived. It may be that in windy weather or in a downpour they tended to collapse on their users.

---

11   Advertisement of 1715 for collapsible parasols and umbrellas invented by Monsieur Marius. When collapsed they were small enough to fit into a pocket. Marius also invented a square parasol in 1709.

PARAPLUYE
ET PARASOLS
A PORTER DANS LA POCH[E]

LES Parapluyes dont M. Marius a trouvé le secr[et] ne pesent que 5 a 6 onces: ils ne tiennent pas p[lus] de place qu'une petite Ecritoire, & n'embaraff[ent] point la poche; ainfi chacun peut fans s'incommo[der] en avoir un fur foy par précaution contre le mauv[ais] temps. Ils font cependant auffi grands, plus foli[des] refiftent mieux aux grands vents, & fe tendent a[uffi] vite que ceux qui fonten ufage.

C'eft le témoignage que Meffieurs de l'Académie Royale des Sciences m'ont rendu

Cette nouvelle Invention a paru avoir été bien reçue du Public par le grand debit qu[i] fait, ce qui a excité l'Auteur a la perfectionner, au point qu'il ne laiffe plus rien à fouha[iter] côté de la folidité.

A l'egard de ceux qui font ornez, l'on conviendra qu'il ne s'eft encore rien vû en Para[sol] plus agréable pour le goût & la légereté, & que l'on peut contenter en ce genre les Curi[eux] plus difficiles, pour la richeffe des montures & des ornemens. *Il n'y a que pour les marque[s]*

Ils fe font & fe vendent aParis chez M. MARIU[S] demeurant ruë des Foffez Saint Germain, aux trois Entonnoirs.

Par l'autorité d'un Privilège du Roy, portant deffenfe par toute l'étendue du Royaume de l[e] faire, a peine de mille livres d'amende.

Il ne faut pas confondre cet Invention avec celle des Parapluyes dont les branches fe tirent d'un une S[...] Ces fortes de Parapluyes ont depuis par leur pesantes & leur peu de folidité, d'ailleurs il faloit trop de temps pour [...]

1 Parasol cover. Ivory ribbed silk embroidered in gold thread and coloured silks. Italian in origin, mid to late seventeenth century.

2 Two Chinese export parasols. *Left:* ivory handle carved with flowers and leaves, ferrule as a female figure; black silk cover embroidered in silk, faces of ivory; mother-of-pearl rib tips; deep knotted-on fringe; red silk lining; 1840–50. *Right:* ivory handle carved with pagodas and flowers, satin cover embroidered with English flowers in China to Queen Victoria's order, knotted-on fringe, *c.* 1850. This parasol is very similar to one illustrated among the Sangster parasols in the 1851 Exhibition catalogue; both handles are rather old-fashioned for the covers.

3 Parasol covers. *Left:* brown silk woven with bands and bunches of flowers in black silk cut and uncut velvet, knotted-on silk fringe, 1850–60. *Centre:* lavender silk with applied black velvet butterflies, chainstitching and steel beads, elaborately knotted sewn-on fringe, metal frame, pagoda shape, 1860–65. *Right:* white silk woven with yellow roses above festoons of black-and-white flowers, long knotted-on fringe, white silk lining, whalebone frame cased in silk, 1850–60.

4 Queen Victoria's parasols. *Left:* ivory handle carved with feathers and leaves, steel tube stick, solid steel ribs, green silk cover and lining with chainmail interlining, knotted-on fringe. It is not recorded when this parasol was made, but it is likely to have been in the 1840s. *Centre:* diamond-set gunmetal handle, black satin cover trimmed with two flounces of Chantilly lace, lining of thin ruched silk. Inscribed 'Presented to the Queen by Her Majesty's Oldest Parliamentary Subject, C. P. Villiers, June 20th 1897'. *Right:* chased gold and enamel gem-set handle, rectangular-section gilt ribs, pink moiré cover edged with Honiton applied lace. Marked 'Royal Victoria, I. A. Boss, Patentee,' *c.* 1851. Has a velvet-covered box.

3

1750-1840

PARASOLS

In her diary for 1777 Abigail Gawthern of Nottingham noted: 'Used a parasol for the first time, Jun. 15; Mrs Launder bought it in town (London), and one for herself; they were just begun to be used there, and they were the *first* in Nottingham.'[1] She gives no further detail, but the *Westminster Magazine* noticed 'a silk umbrella, or what the French call a Parisol. It is fastened in the middle of a long, japanned walking cane with an ivory crook head. It opens by a spring, and is pushed towards the head of the cane when expanded for use.'[2] This described what was later termed the 'staff parasol' and is probably what the Marchioness Grey meant when she wrote to her eldest daughter in 1777: 'Your sister would be glad to have from Tunbridge a Genteel Umbrella and Walking Stick together.'[3] The paucity of references to parasols hides its origins, but it does seem as if this is the first fashionable use of the parasol in England.

Few such parasols survive. Of the two in the Victoria & Albert Museum, one has a plain stick, a small bone hook, a green silk cover, and whalebone ribs; the other is inlaid with mother-of-pearl, has a bone cylindrical top, and a green silk cover edged with fringe. These parasols echo the tall cane which was a fashionable female accessory of the 1770s and 1780s. Both seem particularly suited to accompany the fashionable *bergère* costume of a looped-up skirt over a short petticoat; indeed, they may have developed as a playful allusion to the shepherd's crook. Staff parasols continued into the 1790s. A fashion plate of 1779[4] (fashion plates were just starting to come into general use, usually in almanacs such as the *Ladies' Complete Pocket Book*, or the *Ladies' Museum or Complete Pocket Memorandum Book*) showed a parasol with a dress very similar to fig. 12 but worn with a more elaborate hat. Continental fashion books, such as the *Journal des Luxus und der Moden*, in the 1780s also showed this type of parasol, sometimes with a knob instead of the hook and a dagged edge to the cover. Some covers were banded both near the centre and at the edge. Even when the handle was short the parasol, when closed, was invariably carried with the rib tips downwards.

12 Staff parasol of green silk, banded with white at the edge, cane stick with small bone hook, and whalebone ribs, 1775–1800, complementing a painted cream silk polonaise dress of the late 1770s. The staff parasol (a later term) seems to have come into fashion about 1777 and remained popular to the early 1790s.

ECCENTRICITIES, MONSTROSITIES, or Bell's and Beau's of 1799.

13 Eccentricities, Monstrosities, or Belles and Beaus of 1799, *by Isaac Cruikshank. The small parasol with the 'marquise' hinge (so that it could be tilted vertically), as it first appears in England.*

The first parasol in America seems to have been imported direct from India to Baltimore in 1772, and caused consternation when first used.[5] Not much later, the fashion reached Philadelphia. 'They were then scouted in the public *Gazette* as a ridiculous effeminacy. On the other hand, the physicians recommended them to keep off vertigoes, epilepsies, sore eyes, fevers etc.'[6]

Men did not, as a rule, carry parasols. Although Mrs Montagu, writing from Bath in 1780, mentioned 'the *Macaronis* who trip in pumps and with Parasols over their heads', she later writes of a Miss taking an umbrella to protect herself from the noon sun, and may have just interchanged the two terms.[7] Men, however, did carry umbrellas as sunshades. The valetudinarian Mr Phippen, 'a martyr to dyspepsia', in *The Dead Secret* by Wilkie Collins, used 'the lightest umbrella he could pick out of the hall' in 1844; it had a hook handle.[8] Even 'Laurie' Laurence in Louisa M. Alcott's *Good Wives* carried an

umbrella in Nice in the 1860s. Ecru-coloured sunshades lined with dark green, for tropical use by men and women in the late nineteenth century, were known as 'sun umbrellas'.

Parasols had remained fashionable in France since the beginning of the century. Madame de Pompadour, mistress of Louis XV, and the arbiter of taste, possessed Chinese sunshades. Parasols are depicted more often in France than in England. In the engraving *Le Rendez-vous pour Marly*, 1777,[9] by Jean Michel Moreau the Younger (1741–1814), for instance, the parasol depicted is long-handled but not of the staff parasol type, and the shallow pagoda-shaped cover is edged with a little frill. There are no stretchers, nor are there any on a very similar parasol in the *Delights of Maternity*, 1776,[10] by the same artist. Both might be non-collapsible or have short stretchers between the ribs and the central curve of the cover, part of an automatic opening device referred to in the *Encyclopédie Méthodique*. Nicklaus Wilhelm von Heideloff (1761–1839) showed similar parasols without stretchers in the *Gallery of Fashion*, published in England between 1794 and 1802.

From being very large, the parasol became very small just before 1800. A cartoon by Isaac Cruikshank, George

27

Cruikshank's father, lampooning fashions for 1799, shows a short-handled, small-diameter parasol with a cover that could be tilted to lie parallel to the stick. This style was later called 'marquise', presumably after the Marquise de Pompadour (1721–64) but although it could have existed in the middle of the century – table-tops hinged like this were well known then – this appears to be its first depiction. It was a construction best suited to small-diameter parasols.

Most surviving examples of this type of parasol, sometimes called fan parasols because they resemble the cockade fan, have turned wood sticks and green silk covers (see fig. 14). From 1807 onwards the stick appears to be plain with no turning, and is sometimes quite long. In the Museum of London is a parasol which belonged to Queen Charlotte, consort of George III. It has a folding stick of cane, capped at each end with gold engraved with 'CR' under a crown; the runner is gold on ivory and bears the London hallmark for 1814–15; the ribs are whalebone. At some period the original cover has been replaced by one of blue moiré trimmed with lace, perhaps for Queen Victoria.

In the first decade of the nineteenth century some parasols were trimmed with fringe, short at first, becoming quite long about 1809, often criss-crossed in lattice pattern echoing the fringes found on contemporary furniture and curtains. From fashion plates it appears that parasols had 8, 10, 12 or 16 ribs. Descriptions are few, but a quilted parasol of shaded silk, lined with white satin, was recorded in *La Belle*

14 *Parasol, 1800–1810, green silk on whalebone ribs, with folding stick, and 'marquise' hinge. This is very similar to the parasols that appear in* Eccentricities, Monstrosities, or Belles and Beaus of 1799 *(see fig. 13).*

*15 'London Fashionable Walking and Full Dress',
engraved for the* Lady's Magazine, *1810. The parasol is
white with a lattice fringe (fashionable also on furniture
of the period), and is possibly a pagoda shape. The
handle is probably of turned wood, rather thicker than
in the previous decade.*

Assemblée in 1808, a plaid (checked) parasol in 1810,
and a purple-and-green shot silk matching 'ridicule' and
parasol in August 1811. The latter had a metal-tipped
stick and a tassel hanging from each rib tip. By this date
the parasol was considerably larger than it had been ten
years before, and attempts were made to change its
basic shape. In 1812 a patent was granted to Charles
Price, Umbrella Maker, of the Strand, London, for an
'Imperial Solumbra'.[11] The drawing accompanying a
rather confused text shows an ornate stick with a square
crook handle, a cover with a lattice fringe, and ribs bent
upwards at the ends in a 'Chinese' pagoda shape and
held there, it seems, by springs through the ribs. It was
probably unsuccessful, for it does not appear in fashion
plates, but by 1809[12] the ordinary pagoda or 'Chinese'
shape, forming an ogee or Tudor arch in profile, had

arrived and was to remain in fashion until the end of the
1830s (see fig. 18). The pagoda had ribs joined to the
stick at right-angles and a coiled spring round the stick
above them and under the cover to make the distinctive
shape.

The arrival of the pagoda coincided with growing
elaboration in women's dress, at the bottom of the skirt, at
the top of the sleeves and on the head. Increasingly
fashion was looking over its shoulder, not at classical
Greece and Rome, but at late Gothic Europe. From 1810
to 1820, although dresses retained the high waist, they
acquired 'Tudor' slashed sleeves, and 'Elizabethan' ruffs.
From then on it became a general rule that the size of the
parasol varied in almost direct relationship to the size of
the headgear, not, as one would imagine from its
protective purpose, in inverse ratio. The cover, too, was
often trimmed to harmonize with the dress.

The parasols of the 1810s had turned wooden sticks,
sometimes, especially after 1816, with a half-U-shaped
curved handle. Mrs John Mackie, sketched in Rome by
Ingres in 1816, had such a parasol folded on her lap.[13]
Some had plain covers, others a band of different colour
near the edge, which could be fringed or vandyked; an
ivory ring is the usual method of keeping the parasol
closed. Some of the most magnificent parasols of this
decade have intricately carved ivory sticks imported
from China (see fig. 16). One, in Cheltenham Museum,
has the handle deeply carved with dragons, birds and
clouds, and the stick beyond the silver-plated joint cover
decorated with shallow carving of flowers and leaves. It
belonged to a member of the Winnington Ingram family
of Stanford Court, Worcestershire, but, regrettably, has
lost its cover. Towards the end of the decade the stick
became much thinner and small hook and crutch
handles appeared. In his caricature *Dandies of 1817,
Monstrosities of 1818* George Cruikshank illustrated
parasols with such extremely thin sticks and long
ferrules that they might easily be mistaken for those of
the 1840s, were it not for the pagoda shape uncommon in
that decade.

The handle had turned raised rings from 1818
onwards and twisted decoration throughout the 1820s.
Imitation bamboo with small hooks of bone or ivory,
similar to the umbrellas of the period, appeared in 1827.
The straight and the hook forms continued; sometimes
the latter was held downwards as if the possessor was
about to play hockey! Large curved hook handles were
fashionable in 1828, the end sometimes trumpet-shaped
or carved as a bird's head. Ferrules were often long. The
covers were a little more elaborate, often with a damask
band in a different colour near the edge. In 1821 the most
elegant parasols had covers with a feather-stitched
border trimmed with Mechlin lace, a shot blue-and-

white lining, and the stick and handle 'of polished steel, the thick part . . . beautifully wrought and the handle like the leaf of the acanthus'.[14] Steel jewellery was very fashionable that year. In August 1824 the *Ladies' Monthly Museum* announced that 'the newest parasols are of Lyonese silk and of a lilac colour'. In the previous January customs duties on imported silks had been drastically reduced, bounties on whale, herring and other fisheries were to expire, and 'a number of fancy articles and articles of dress, which are now prohibited, and furnish

16 Parasol handle of 1810–20; Chinese turned ivory stick carved with pagodas, houses, trees and flowers, and silver gilt hinge cover chased with laurel leaves. The cover is pink silk, lined with white. A fringe is probably missing.

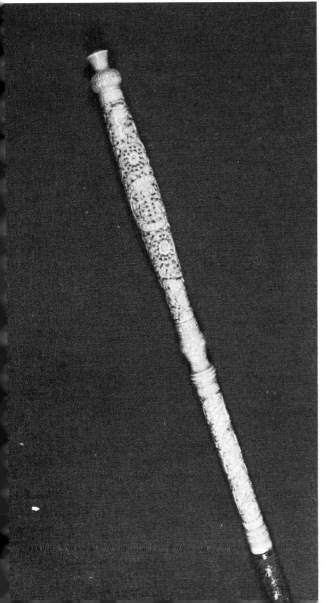

17 Fashion plate, 'Marine Costume' from La Belle Assemblée, *July 1826: a round dress of fine India muslin trimmed with lace and embroidery and worn with a hat of white* gros de Naples *trimmed with lace and tulips. The parasol is not described, but is coloured green. The handle is probably of turned wood, with the small hook that is characteristic of the decade.*

the trade of the French smugglers, are to be admitted on a payment of 30 per cent *ad valorem*'.[15] Parasols were not mentioned specifically but even then, as for much of the nineteenth century, the most fashionable articles of dress came from Paris, although occasionally Mrs John Bull rebelled against this, and occasionally, too, the tide flowed in the other direction.

In 1826 fashionable parasols were neither lined nor fringed, the whalebone ribs had mother-of-pearl tips, and the *gros de Naples* covers were white, hermit-brown or bottle-green (elsewhere myrtle was held to be the only green becoming to the complexion). The handle was a carved mother-of-pearl hand grasping an ebony bar.[16] Sea-green parasols were generally adopted with morning visiting dresses and at the seaside; the whalebone ribs were rounded into little knobs or had brass tips like umbrellas. In 1828 some parasols were trimmed with contrasting fringe but some 'are much larger than they were seen last year, being of a dark colour and bearing no fringe, they answer the double purpose of an umbrella'.[17] Parasols painted with Chinese and Persian patterns on a white ground, and mounted on bamboo or rosewood sticks were noted in Paris.[18] By 1829 'the new parasols are all fringed',[19] complimenting the fringe that was becoming fashionable on dresses. Contrasting colours were noted, including milk-chocolate lined with sea-green.

The parasols of the 1820s had been carried over dresses that had expansive skirts and sleeves, especially after 1825 when the waist level had returned to its natural position. Both hats and bonnets were wide-brimmed at the sides. The 1830s continued the trend; skirts and sleeves became larger. Wide brims continued for hats, but bonnets, which were becoming increasingly fashionable, had brims arching over the forehead and caught tight to the side of the head by ribbons tied beneath the chin.

The commonly used adjective for parasols of this period is 'large', meaning about 38 inches in length, and about 36 inches in diameter when open. Handles of wood or ivory are often elaborately carved. Hooks are angular, often made in two pieces; the upright and a bar which screws on to it at right angles (many of the ivory examples have become loose and are now missing). T-shaped bars, especially in wood, appeared in the fashion plates of 1832 and 1833. Smaller hooks were fashionable in 1834.

The brass stick often folds and the joint with the handle frequently has a brass collar stamped with such decorative motifs as 'London' under a crown between

18 Parasol, 1830–40: carved ivory handle and ferrule, ivory tips to the eight whalebone ribs, lacquered iron stretchers, brass stick, hinge cover embossed with a crown and 'London' above palm leaves, ring closure of ivory, and green silk cover in pagoda shape. Length 38 inches; diameter when open 34 inches.

19   The Revd D'Ewes Coke, his wife Hannah, and Daniel Parker Coke, MP, c. 1782, by Joseph Wright of Derby. The short umbrella is green with a turned wood stick, brass ring and runner; the ribs do not seem to have any added tips.

palm fronds, the Royal Arms in a wreath of roses, thistles and shamrock, or even Brighton Pavilion with its domes and titled *Brighton Palace*. (As this was William IV's term for his brother's creation rather than George IV's own, these parasols would seem to date from after 1830; they were probably seaside souvenirs.) The pagoda was still fashionable and green still a popular colour – the voters of Eatanswill in *The Posthumous Papers of the Pickwick Club* were bribed with 'five-and-forty green parasols, at seven and sixpence a-piece' for their wives[20] – and *gros de Naples* was still a fashionable fabric, though others such as foulard and moiré were appearing. A parasol of white moiré was carried with a grey pelisse for 'public promenade dress' in September 1833.[21] Some seem to have had a band of lace or transparent material as a border. Mrs Bloss, a wealthy widow in one of the *Sketches by Boz* (1836–7) carried with a pelisse and bonnet 'the colour of the interior of a damson pie' a green parasol 'with a cobweb border'.[22]

Sleeves shrank abruptly in 1836, becoming tight at the upper arm. As bonnets were already tight to the sides of the head, the large parasol looked out of proportion. In about 1836 a smaller folding parasol was introduced particularly for carriage use; its smaller size and shape was to dominate the history of the parasol for the next thirty-five or so years.

UMBRELLAS

In about 1750 Jonas Hanway (1712–86), philanthropist and traveller, started to carry an umbrella regularly whilst walking in London. During his lifetime he saw the acceptance of the umbrella as a gentleman's accessory. It was even nicknamed a 'Hanway', and, perhaps not surprisingly, he was later credited with its invention. Although umbrellas were known they must have been uncommon, for Lt Colonel James Wolfe (the General Wolfe killed at the battle of Quebec in 1759) wrote to his father from Paris on 4 December 1752:

> The people here use umbrellas in hot weather to defend them from the sun, and something of the same kind to secure them from the snow and rain. I wonder that a practice so useful is not introduced into England where there are such frequent showers, and especially in the country, where they can be expanded without any inconveniency.[23]

Hanway's umbrella was a foreign one; it had a handle of ebony carved or inlaid with fruits and flowers, a pale-green silk cover and stone-coloured satin lining.[24] It folded up into 'the length of a man's hand'. Though often in delicate health, Hanway carried the umbrella more to protect his clothes than his person. His biographer, John Pugh wrote of him:

As it was frequently necessary for him to appear in polite circles on unexpected occasions, he usually wore dress clothes with a large French bag wig. His hat, ornamented with a gold button, was of a size and fashion to be worn as well under the arm as on the head. When it rained, a small parapluie defended his face and wig; thus he was always prepared to enter into any company without impropriety or the appearance of negligence.[25]

20 Umbrella, 1780–1800. Turned stick which is jointed and also unscrews into two parts, nine hinged whalebone ribs, green silk cover. Runner inscribed 'Hodges, No. 14 John Street, Adelphi' (probably the owner, as the Adelphi was an exclusive housing development designed by Robert Adam). The cord was to prevent the umbrella turning inside out in a high wind.

It is possible that Hanway's umbrella was French, for not only did Marius's umbrellas fold in this way forty-odd years before, but a collapsible umbrella is illustrated in Diderot's *Encyclopédie* of 1763. A folding umbrella of that type is in the Welsh Folk Museum (see fig. 20). It is very similar to one in the portrait of the Revd and Mrs Thomas Gisborne, 1786, by Joseph Wright of Derby.

These small umbrellas for the use of gentlemen went side-by-side with umbrellas which, according to *The Report of the Juries of the Great Exhibition* of 1851, 'closely resemble the ordinary gig-umbrella of the present day'. These gig-umbrellas survive in quantity, as they have been made over a considerable period. They were advertised in the Junior Army and Navy Stores catalogue for 1894 from 6s. 6d. to 35s., with eight to twelve cane, whalebone or Fox's Paragon ribs; and as Scotch Gingham Umbrellas from 4s. 6d. to 18s. 6d. each in Gamage's catalogue for 1913. They are very durable and are favoured by auctioneers of livestock; two have been seen in use during the past year. Most have one-inch-thick sticks with ovoid 'pine' head handles turned with concave bands, cane ribs, and brass tips. Wired to the stick is often a brass cap with a hinged ring at the ferrule end, and there is a black or green cotton cover, with cords woven in near the edge. Some have ventilating caps at the top to prevent the umbrella from turning inside-out in high wind. Dating of them can only be approximate, depending on the presence of machine-stitching or the decoration on the inside cap. Such umbrellas were also kept in the entrance halls of houses for servants to use when escorting guests to and from carriages.

Despite the example of Jonas Hanway, it took at least twenty years for the umbrella to become established. This was due, in part, to snobbishness. In 1768 the Marquis Caraccioli commented of Paris that although it had long been the custom never to go out without an umbrella, 'those who wish not to be confounded with the vulgar, prefer to run the risk of getting wet to be regarded as people who walk on foot, for the umbrella is the sign of having no carriage'.[26]

Umbrellas were more used by men in France than in England. Horace Walpole suggested in a letter that this was so they need not wear hats and spoil their wigs.[27]

---

21 Gig umbrella, 1860–1900: black painted wood stick ▷ with 'pine cone' handle; black cotton cover, corded at edge; nine cane ribs with brass tips. This is an umbrella of the traditional sort which was kept in hallways to shelter visitors from the carriage to the door. Length 42½ inches; rib length 33½ inches; diameter when open 56½ inches.

Hairdressers carried umbrellas to protect the wigs which were the advertisements of their trade, and one is so depicted by the caricaturist Bunbury in 1771.[28] A French visitor to London noted that 'it is a rule with the people of London not to use, or suffer foreigners to use, our umbrellas of taffeta or waxed silk'.[29] Umbrellas were so much associated with foreigners that in 1778 a London footman, John Macdonald, using one that he had acquired in Spain, was jeered at as a Frenchman and became known as 'Beau Macdonald' or the 'Scotch Frenchman'.[30] Gradually, however, public opinion was changing. In 1766 a Mr Heath began to import umbrellas from Genoa and they became fashionable in Exeter, in spite of being unmanageable in windy weather.[31] In June 1768 an American paper, the *Boston Evening Post* carried an advertisement for Isaac Greenwood, Turner, who made and sold 'neat mahogany frames tipt with ivory or brass ferrils, 32s. 6d. plain, others at 40s.; printed at 36s.; neat Persian Umbrellas compleat at 6s. and 10s. and in proportion for better silk'.[32] He and other Boston traders advertised frames and sometimes a fabric-cutting service for ladies who wanted to make their own covers; but this might refer more to parasols.

Most of the mentions of umbrellas as a novel accessory for men in Britain occur in the 1770s and 1780s. The first umbrella in Stamford was a large green silk one 'apparently of Chinese manufacture' bought from Scotland between 1770 and 1780.[33] The first in Sawbridgeworth, Hertfordshire, had been brought back from Leghorn in 1775 or 1776.[34] Mrs Gaskell in *Cranford*, a fictionalized account of her own young womanhood in Knutsford, Cheshire, recalled the tradition of the first umbrella that had been seen there; its user had been mobbed by little boys who had called it 'a stick in petticoats'. She also mentioned 'a magnificent family red silk umbrella under which a gentle little spinster . . . used to patter to church on rainy days . . . It might have been held up by a strong father over a troop of little ones; the poor little lady – the survivor of all – could scarcely carry it.' A red silk umbrella from Leghorn was reported in Bristol in 1780,[35] perhaps part of a stock of 'silk and other umbrellas' advertised in a local newspaper in 1775. By 1784, it would seem from the cartoon accompanying the essay *A Battle of Umbrellas* in the *Wit's Magazine*, all the world carried umbrellas – men, women and children! In the 1780s there were obviously some umbrellas of British manufacture, for Thomas Folgham, of 112 Cheapside, London, advertised in 1787 'a great assortment of his much approved pocket and portable umbrellas, which for lightness, elegance and strength, far exceed anything of the kind ever imported or manufactured in this kingdom. All kinds of common umbrellas prepared in a particular way, that will never stick together.'[36] In

22 A View from Knightsbridge Barracks, *1817,* by Richard Dighton: a caricature of Captain Horace Seymour who is wearing a black top hat, brown coat and grey trousers, and carries a green umbrella. The brass spike and rib tips can be clearly seen; also the end of what appears to be a long runner.

1786 John Beale, Umbrella Maker, of City Road, Middlesex, had taken out a patent for a 'pockett spring umbrella that opens by its own action' which had a cranked stick. This was the first patent granted for an umbrella, another sign of its popularity. There were many statements to reinforce this impression. John Macdonald, the London footman, wrote in 1790: 'Now it is become a great trade in London and a very useful branch of business.' In 1810 the *Universal Magazine* commented that the umbrella 'is now made of such cheap materials that it is in the hands of every class'.[37] According to Dr Cleland, 'every child at school, mechanic, and servant is provided with an umbrella'.[38]

In 1811 an umbrella was a silent witness in the case against Richard Gurney for alienating the affections of a Mrs Muskett from her husband.[39] Umbrellas were seen during rain at the siege of Bayonne in 1813 in the

Peninsula War, and provoked Wellington into castigating his officers: 'Lord Wellington does not approve the use of umbrellas during the enemy's firing, and will not allow the Gentlemen's Sons to make themselves ridiculous in the eyes of the army.' It was the context rather than the umbrella that he disapproved of, for a few days later he remarked to Colonel Tyling: 'The Guards may in uniform when on duty at St James's carry them if they please, but not in the field.'[40] Captain Horace Seymour is shown with an umbrella tucked under one arm in 1817 (see fig. 22). The everyday character of the umbrella is underlined by Admiral Croft's remark to Anne Elliot in *Persuasion*, written by Jane Austen in 1816: '"You can slip in from the shrubbery at any time. And there you will find we keep our umbrellas, hanging up by that door. A good place, is it not? But . . . you will not think it a good place, for yours were always kept in the butler's room."'[41] Captain Wentworth, in the same novel, equipped himself properly for Bath by buying an umbrella.[42]

Umbrellas of this period have cane or whalebone ribs with brass tips; steel stretchers with pitchfork ends, often varnished or pickled to look like brass; a wood or metal stick, often with a brass conical ferrule, sometimes with a ball at the end; and a wood-and-ivory, antler or walrus-tusk cross handle. The cover, of silk in best-quality umbrellas, and cotton in cheaper ones, was usually green, but could be blue, red or brown. Structurally the most important developments came in the form of the top notch in the 1820s. Until then the brass-capped ribs were attached to the stick by wire. Friction on the wire made the umbrella clumsy to open and weakened it at this point. In 1821 Samuel Hobday of Birmingham was granted a patent for improvements to the umbrella frame, including the substitution of the wire by a T-shaped bar, a ball joint, or a hook, all of which worked in a special top notch. The umbrella in the patent drawings has an antler handle above a straight section with an oval hole for a tasselled cord, and a band decorated with Tudor roses. An umbrella very similar to this, marked

23 Premium, Par & Discount, 1822, by I. & G. Cruikshank: three different types of umbrella, the fashionable, the family and the everyday. All are large with only a short distance between the rib tips and the handle, and above the spike on the umbrella on the right is a leather washer which protrudes, a feature of many umbrellas in the first half of the nineteenth century.

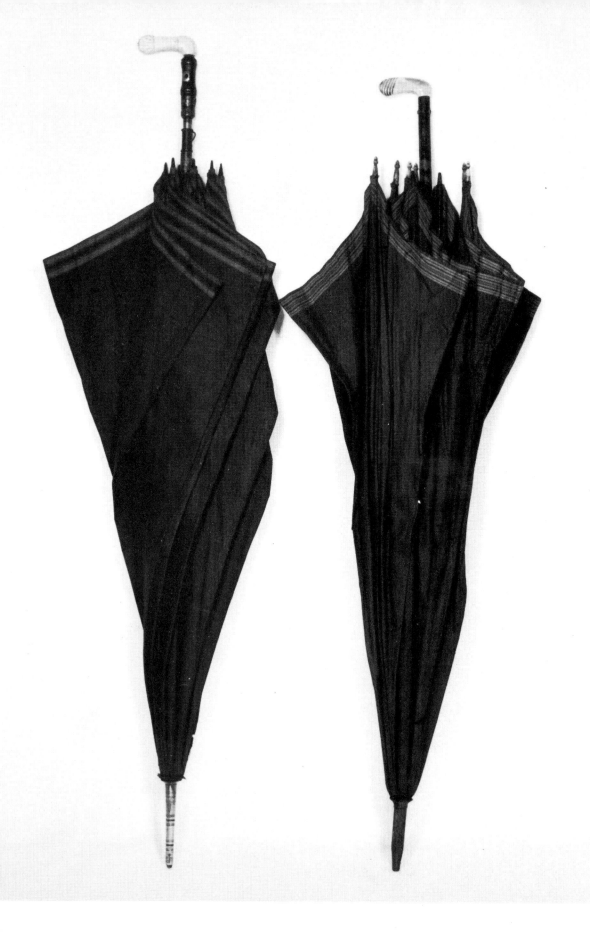

Hobday, Francis & Co., Royal Letters Patent on the runner, is in the Museum of London (see fig. 32).

Both Francis Deakin's patent of 1823 and John Hopper Caney's patent of 1829 concerned top notches. In Deakin's patent the rib had a brass cap cast with a dovetailed joint; in Caney's patent a wire through a hole in the brass cap. The wire had wedge ends and fitted securely under a brass disc. Caney also invented a git so that the stretcher could be attached beneath the rib, not through it. Luke Hébert, author of *The Engineer's and Mechanic's Encyclopaedia* (1833) considered these inventions crucial to the history of the umbrella, but neither was suitable for mass production and they were superseded by Samuel Fox's Paragon frame in the 1850s. Most early-nineteenth-century umbrellas have long runners, 6 inches long in some cases, and only a short distance, 4–6 inches, from the rib tips when closed to the top of the handle. During the late 1820s and 1830s, however, the runner became shorter.

Although the cross handle continued in fashion past the middle of the century – fashions in umbrellas were much slower to change than those of parasols – there were others. In 1830 the *Gentleman's Magazine of Fashion* stated that 'The Umbrella of the man of fashion is of myrtle-green *gros de Naples* without any kind of border at the edge; handle of Chinese laurel without any head, only a simple plate of gold.' During his exile in Caen in 1832, however, George 'Beau' Brummell had 'a brown silk umbrella, which was always protected by a silk case that fitted as accurately as his own coat'. The handle was an unflattering portrait of 'George IV carved in ivory, with a well-curled wig and smiling graciously'. Until that time he had always carried a cane.[43] Another umbrella with a carved ivory head handle, said to be a portrait of the first Duke of Wellington, is in the Cheltenham Museum. The cane stick is in three parts and screws together; the whalebone ribs fold at the gits

---

24 Umbrellas, 1830–40. Left: *ivory handle, mahogany stem with brass-mounted hole, long brass runner embossed with flowers, whalebone ribs, brass tubular stick, green cotton cover banded near the edge, and brass spike. Length 37 inches; diameter when open 45 inches.* Right: *bone handle, cane stick, brass-mounted hole, whalebone ribs with bone tips, green cotton cover banded near the edge, open cap, and unadorned spike. Bought in London or Leicester and used in the village of Market Overton, where its owner was a constable. Length 35 inches; diameter when open 45 inches. Note the short distance between the rib tips and the handle.*

and the steel runner slides right to the end of the stick, held in place by two sets of springs. Unfortunately the cover is missing.

By the end of the 1830s the umbrella was so universally used that it even had its own social distinctions. In Dickens's *Sketches by Boz*, published in 1836–7, Mr Minns, a precise bachelor of forty-eight with a Government position and his own income, had a brown silk umbrella with an ivory handle; a lawyer from the Temple a green umbrella and a blue bag; and Islington clerks 'with large families and small salaries' disdained to carry their 'once green cotton umbrellas', on a sunny day. From the turn of the century umbrella users had been a source of ridicule. In *Hints to the Bearers of Walking Sticks and Umbrellas* (1801), J.S. Duncan categorized them as mostly 'sky-strikers' or 'mud-scoopers': 'Every passer-by either jerks up his Umbrella to the sky, whereby the shorter endangers with the points of his whalebone the eyes of the taller, or dashes it to the ground so as to impede all passage.' Graphic illustrations point out the dangers. In 1825 John Liston, the actor, portrayed the character 'Paul Pry' with what came to be described as 'a ubiquitous umbrella', and the catchphrase 'I hope I don't intrude.' Revivals of the play kept the character alive to the end of the century, his costume virtually unchanged, and in the 1820s the *World of Fashion* carried a monthly feature, 'Paul Pry in London'. However, the most famous umbrella carrier of the period is Sairey Gamp, the nurse in *Martin Chuzzlewit* (published 1843–4), by Charles Dickens. Her umbrella is a 'species of gig-umbrella . . . in colours like a folded leaf, except where a circular patch of lively blue had been dextrously let in at the top', and 'as something of great price and rarity was displayed with particular ostentation' beside her fireplace.[44] It has a hook handle (probably antler, to judge from the illustration by H.K. Browne) and a brass nozzle. In spite of its baggy appearance it must have originally been an expensive one. Sairey Gamp gave her name to a particularly large and misshapen umbrella, but her surname may have derived from *guingamp*, the French for gingham and the name of a town in Brittany. There is little, if any, discernible difference between men's and women's umbrellas. In 'The History of an Umbrella' in the *World of Fashion*, March 1828, a purple silk umbrella is owned successively by a young lady of fashion, a footman, a bankrupt, a dramatic author, a student, and a seller of newspaper advertisements. The woman addressing a fish seller in *Sketches of Character* by W.J. White (1818) holds an umbrella that is indistinguishable from a man's; and it is conjectural who owned the umbrella in fig. 19.

4

1840-1875

PARASOLS

The accession of Queen Victoria in 1837 coincided with one fashion and inspired another. Sleeves, which had been huge in the early 1830s, became tight to the upper arm, and later became tight altogether, symbolic of a more restrictive era. In 1838 the *World of Fashion* announced the arrival of the 'Victoria parasols for open carriages'; a reintroduction of the marquise parasols of the early years of the century. They were 'perfectly calculated for the purpose, of a very small size, and with folding sticks so that they may be used to shade the face as a fan, they are composed of *poult de soie chinée*. Some are trimmed with fringes, others have an embroidered border – all are pretty.'[1] The sticks were of carved ivory of 'antique patterns'. The *New Belle Assemblée* commented grudgingly in May 1839: 'they are useful for an open carriage, but I do not see any other superiority they possess'. Open carriages became more popular, as they improved in construction. In the 1830s Luke Hopkinson developed the so-called 'English Landau', and Princess Victoria gave her name to a type of coachman-driven phaeton. The carriage parasol operated in reverse to the Marquis Caraccioli's maxim about the umbrella; possession of one implied that one also had a carriage. To the manufacturer, because its utility was of the smallest, it provided an opportunity for lavish use of labour and materials.

The market for these parasols lay in a burgeoning middle class, to whom, especially the women, appearance expressed social status. This middle class formed a large part of the population of 21 million in Great Britain in 1851. It was reaping the benefits of industrialization, and, essentially urban based, built for itself attractive villas and terraces of houses within reach of shopping centres. It was towards this class, which had money, but perhaps lacked the landed property to spend it upon, that the products of textile and clothing industries were directed, and for whom fashion magazines were written. Novelty and exclusiveness became of prime importance. The patent laws, which covered inventions, were supplemented by the Design of Copyrights Acts, in 1839, amended and expanded in 1842. Among ornamental wares, twelve classes were for clothing and textiles.[2] Of parasol manufacturers, one firm in particular utilized the new legislation. Throughout the 1840s and early 1850s W. & J. Sangster, of 140 Regent Street, London, produced a new design virtually every year, most of them registered. In 1843, for instance, they introduced the 'Pekin' parasol, presumably covered in the popular striped materials;[3] and in 1844 the 'La Sylphide' parasol. The latter had a button near the handle which released a spring within the metal tubular stick, so that the parasol could be collapsed by one hand. This was one of the most popular of Sangsters' models, and a number survive in museums. They sold for 5s. 6d. in 1846 (ordinary brown silk parasols with ivory tips cost about 1s. 9½d.). La Sylphide sticks were made 'in every variety of shape and material', including, in 1845, the 'Claremont', which was half the weight of an ordinary parasol. In 1844 Sangsters also introduced the 'Royal Windsor' and the 'Patent Minaret' parasols (the latter was probably a pagoda shape). The 'Patent Indian' parasol was introduced in 1847; it had a rubber band from rib to rib inside so that no external fitting was needed to keep it closed. In 1849 the 'Patent Swiss' parasol with alpaca covers was introduced.

At the Great Exhibition of 1851, Sangsters showed the La Sylphide parasol as well as models trimmed with feathers, embroidered satins, lace and alpaca. Eleven other British inventors and manufacturers exhibited, including Henry Holland of Birmingham (a patent umbrella frame weighing nine ounces); Wilson and Matheson of Glasgow (a folding umbrella, the handle of which could be used as a walking stick); William Slark of the Burlington Arcade, London (a lady's parasol-whip); and Hargrave, Harrison & Co., Wood Street, London (a registered cycloidal parasol). Lewis and Allenby, Regent Street, London (retailers), showed a parasol with a pinked lining, and others with Irish guipure lace covers. I.A. Boss, of London, exhibited what was probably the 'Royal Victoria' parasol, advertised by Cheek and Marsh, Golden Perch, 182 Oxford Street, London, in 1851.[4] One, which is inscribed: 'Royal Victoria, I.A. Boss, Patentee', was presented to Queen

Victoria. It has a gilded hexagonal stick and a gold handle set with diamonds and decorated with the motto of the Order of the Garter on a blue-enamelled spiral ribbon terminating in a band of rubies and emeralds. The knob at the top is engraved with the royal arms underneath a large topaz. The opening mechanism is an enamelled hand with 'I Govern' in Gothic letters on the cuff, which is pulled downwards to open the metal ribs and stretchers, the ends of which fit into a gem-set crown. Above the pink moiré and satin lace-timmed cover is a gold cornucopia-shaped ferrule. The whole is a masterpiece of the jeweller's and parasol maker's craft (see colour plate 4).

Another of Queen Victoria's parasols is unusual in a different way. Its metal stick and ivory handle are not lavish and the cover is plain emerald-green silk, but between the cover and the lining is a steel chain-mail interlining. It was designed to protect the Queen from assassination, but was probably too heavy to be used with comfort.

These parasols are exceptional. In general the parasols of the early 1840s, like many of the dresses, are

25 'La Sylphide' parasol, 1844–50. Ivory handle, metal stick, brass mount marked 'Royal Patent La Sylphide', puce cover woven with flowers, blue fringe. The button near the mount and the cord of the tassels operates the closing device.

very plain with understated trimmings. Both carriage and small walking parasols have real or imitation rosewood sticks and small handles of mother-of-pearl, ivory or bone, either as a small carved bar, sometimes with a two-dimensional scroll, or a knob. Carriage parasols usually have either a bone or ivory ring, some fixed while others swivel, or a domed fitting at the ferrule; some have a small bell-shaped ferrule. Walking parasols have ferrules of mother-of-pearl or ivory: short and carved, slender versions of those of the 1820s and 1830s; or long and thin, especially towards the end of the 1840s. Some, however, have a fixed ring, occasionally lyre-shaped. In contrast to the previous decades the quantity and quality of the ivory and the carving is much poorer. In part this may be due to the Opium Wars with

China, but also to mass production. Ribs are whalebone or cheaply imitated in cane. Hinge covers on carriage parasols are brass, japanned, or less often silver- or nickel-plated. The shape in general varies from an inverted saucer to a shallow dome, although pagodas are also seen, and range from the very small (called the parasolette in 1842) to the large.

Covers are various: white *gros de Naples* spotted and edged with pink in 1839, Pekin in 1843, cameleon (silk shot with three colours) in 1844, satins both plain and with patterned borders, and 'moirés, glacés and brocaded silks'[5] in 1846. An advertisement of 1843 records: '154 dozen rich brown silk parasols, rich borders and pearl tips at 2s. 6½d., a lot of Green and Drab ditto at 12½d.'[6] Covers might be lace-trimmed: 'lace and embroidered borders continue to be the favourite trimmings for dress. The former, indeed, is in high vogue – lace parasols, lace fans, lace shawls and lace mantles being everywhere the rage.'[7] It would seem, however, from illustrations, that 'lace parasols' had covers trimmed with lace, rather than made entirely of lace, although guipure covers appeared in 1849. Fringe returned as a trimming in 1839 but was most fashionable from 1844; it was short, no more that two inches in depth until later in the decade. The

26 Unusual-shaped covers. Left: small ivory hook handle, carved ferrule, wood stick, cover of blue-and-pink shot silk woven in chessboard pattern, knotted-on pink-and-blue fringe, white silk lining. The ribs are bent near the tips, and it is possibly an automatic opener; runner marked 'Royal Windsor, Reg. 13th Feby 1844'. Right: ivory handle carved with a greyhound's head, brass joint cover, twelve solid steel 10-inch ribs, blue silk cover trimmed with Bedfordshire Maltese lace, and knotted-on blue-and-white silk fringe. Runner marked 'Patent Stella, Regd. 30 Dec. 1850'; the ribs and the shape of the cover make a star shape.

Ladies' Gazette of Fashion, in July 1847, reported of some parasols with two rows of fringe; 'the top row narrower than the second; the first row is that of the colour of the parasol, the second that of the lining, the effect is equally pretty and pleasing'. In about 1847, some covers were cut with curves between the rib tips, rather than the straight hem or selvedge hitherto used, and this fashion continued into the 1850s.

Green and brown continued as popular colours from the 1830s but, towards the end of the 1840s, strong shades of pink and blue became fashionable.[8] In fact as the 1840s ended and the 1850s began there seemed to be a general feeling of optimism, confirmed by the Great Exhibition of 1851, and a blossoming in fabrics, trimmings and styles of dress. These became more marked as the 1850s progressed, displayed over the steel hoops of the crinoline, which appeared in 1856. Dowdy colours and understatement were shunned. In 1848 a lady writing to the *Art Union* magazine complained of the dreariness of the brown parasol and suggested something on the lines of flowers instead. The result in 1850 was 'the Floriform Parasol, which exhibits, when open, the elegant outline of an expanded flower'.[9] This is the spirit of the 1850s.

Although large parasols are referred to both at the beginning and at the end of the 1840s, there are two types which seem stylistically and technically to belong to the years around 1850. Two in the Museum of Costume in Bath are very similar. Both have white silk covers; one is painted with Chinese subjects, the other with European scenes in Chinese style. Both have japanned iron wire ribs, one white, the other black; and iron sticks, one white, the other tortoiseshell. Each has a spring with a hook at each end mounted on a long runner; the hooks clip over rings on the stick. Such a spring appears in an advertisement of 1839 by M. Cazal, a famous French manufacturer who exhibited at the Great Exhibition, but

27   Parasol, 1850–55: silk painted with scenes and flowers in the Chinese style, metal stick painted to resemble tortoiseshell, black-japanned ribs, ivory tips, ivory handle carved as a greyhound, and spring with hooks at both ends. Probably French.

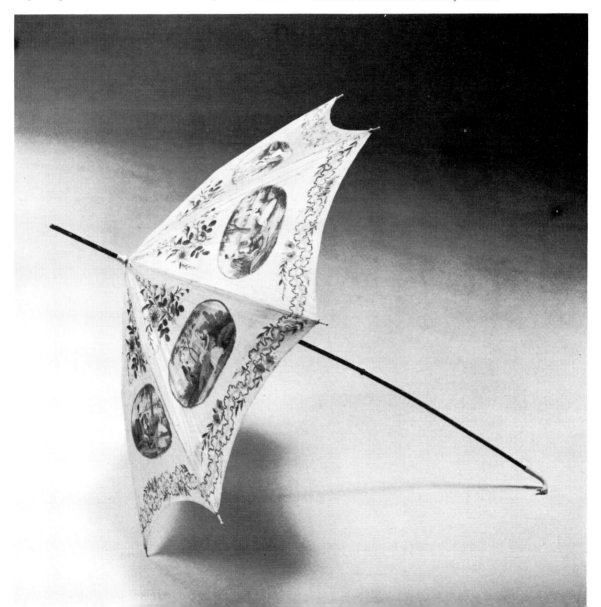

a similar spring was patented by I.A. Boss in 1845. Both these parasols have the slenderness typical of the 1840s and an elegance which could be French. Automatic-opening parasols with similar frames but two sets of stretchers probably belong to this era too. In 1852 John Gedge advertised 'The Registered Self-Opening Umbrella and Parasol'[10] from Paris; and large parasols with thin sticks appear in French fashion plates.[11] Other large parasols have Chinese ivory handles, sometimes hooked, elaborately carved with dragons and land-scapes in traditional style. The silk covers are lavishly embroidered. Two examples in the Victoria & Albert Museum belonged to Queen Victoria. One was embroidered in China with English flowers to her order; the other has embroidered bands of pansies, laurel leaves and roses, and a floral triangle on each gore. According to tradition, it was carried by the Queen on a visit to the Great Exhibition. A third example, in the same museum, is embroidered with Chinese figures with faces of painted ivory, in the manner of the 'hundred faces' Chinese fans imported at this period (see colour plate 2). The *Ladies' Cabinet* reported in 1850: 'There is a profusion of embroideries on all materials this year.'

For the next fifteen years the carriage parasol changes only in detail and it is often difficult to date a particular model, especially when it may have been re-covered. Expensive parasols, would of course, be used for more than one season, whereas cheaper ones could be discarded after one summer. In general, carriage parasols are more elaborate than walking parasols.

28   *Parasol handles.* Left to right: *1820–40: carved ivory, brass handle mount stamped with a crown and flowers, cover of green damask, on a walking-length parasol. 1845–50: ivory carved with a hook handle as a human hand holding a ball, band carved with pears, on a walking-length parasol. 1840–50: carved mother-of-pearl, wood stick, on a walking-length parasol. 1865–75: ivory handle carved with fruits and flowers, silver-plated band, on a carriage parasol. 1870–75: ivory handle carved with acanthus leaf scrolls and festoons of flowers, ivory hinge cover, on a carriage parasol.*

29   *Sangsters' parasols exhibited at the Great*   ▷
Exhibition, 1851, from the official catalogue. As these are exhibition pieces, the handles and the ferrules are more elaborately carved than usual, and the covers are embroidered.

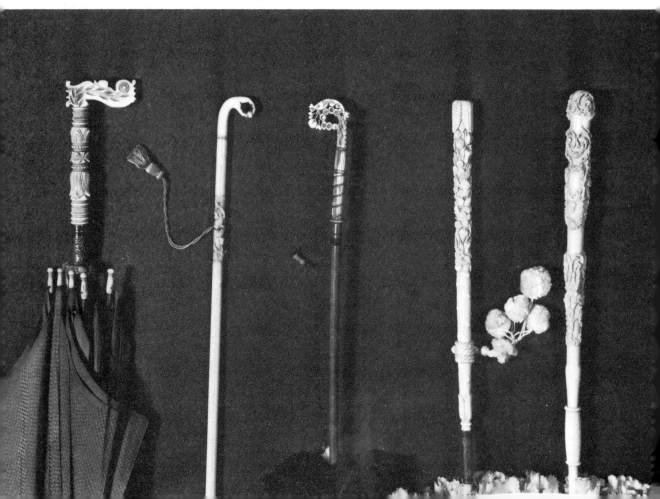

Throughout the period the sticks and handles of carriage parasols are usually of ivory or wood, and the hinge covers of brass or plated on brass, or of ivory, when stick and handle are both ivory. Sticks are very thin, about three-eighths of an inch in diameter. Handles, which are either small ball- or pear-shaped knobs, small hooks with spurs, or variations of the crutch handle (from 1847), are often very elaborate in the 1850s, with bands of chip carving, and spiral turning. They became plainer in the 1860s, the turning dwindling to a series of knobs, or a diaper of small lumps rather like holly or blackthorn sticks, the latter sometimes tipped with tiny domes of red coral if the handle is ivory. The hook handles lost their spurs and became mere carved bars. Towards the end of the 1860s handles and sticks became thicker, often club-shaped, sometimes with a bump behind. Thin ivory handles elaborately carved with wreaths of flowers, fruiting vines, or cords which appear to pass in and out of the solid, would seem to belong to the end of the 1850s and 1860s. To this period also probably belong the carved Italian coral handles. One in the Welsh Folk Museum is carved as a female figure with a feather headdress; another at Bath has a twiggy loop of coral,

and a third in the Gallery of English Costume, Manchester, has the ferrule as well as the handle carved as female figures. The sticks of these parasols are often ivory and the fittings of silver or silver-gilt. The covers, too, are rich; silk covered with lace, Chantilly in one example; black-and-white Irish tatting in another. One charming feature of these rare parasols is the rib tips; they are also of coral, carved as dogs' heads, eagles' heads, and human hands holding balls suspended from rings.

Although whalebone and cane were still used for ribs, there was a third choice: steel. It was used at first for best-quality parasols and later became universal. Henry Holland had produced metal tubes for umbrella ribs in 1840, but the metal ribs in most parasols are of solid wire as produced by Samuel Fox & Co. near Sheffield, from 1848 onwards (see fig. 2).

---

30 One-piece cover of printed warp frame fabric, 1855–65. The colour of the centre is brown; the band is printed with motifs similar to those found on the printed shawls of this period.

In the 1850s covers were invariably domed, echoing the line of the skirt, though some shallow pagodas did appear, and were trimmed with fringe up to six inches in depth towards the end of the decade. The commonest type of parasol is covered with puce (purplish-brown) moiré banded with satin near the edge, trimmed with sewn-on long fringe, and has a short bone ferrule with a swivel ring and fringe around the bottom; a varnished or painted wooden stick with a chip-carved handle, ending in a small hook with a spur; cane ribs wired to the stick; black-japanned steel stretchers and a brass runner. This type of parasol must have been made in large quantities, as so many of them survive even though they are not very strong. Each stretcher is attached through a rib, thus weakening it, the wire joining the ribs to the stick can wear or rust away, and the fringe can become entangled with the tips, endangering the cover and ribs when opening. Moiré appears in all sorts of colours on parasols – blue, green, brown, black – nearly all dark; lighter-coloured moirés were usually teamed with ivory sticks. In the picture *Ramsgate Sands* by W.P. Frith, exhibited at the Royal Academy in 1854, the parasols are either plain or banded with satin near the edge. All the smaller

31   Advertisement from a paper bag, c. 1860: all the parasols have the lumpy turned sticks and the covers with patterned decoration typical of the 1850s.

ones have shallow domes and fringe about four inches in depth, and one is a marquise parasol, a popular style at this period. Two larger ones, which may be umbrellas, are used by the older ladies. This picture also shows the extent to which Victorian women covered themselves up against the sun's rays. All the women and even the little girls wear bonnets, each with an 'ugly' (a silk and cane eye-shade) over the front of it, and they all carry a parasol; the only child with bare feet is paddling.

In addition to silk and cotton a third material, alpaca, was introduced by W. & J. Sangster for covering parasols and umbrellas, in the late 1840s. Alpaca was cheaper than silk, but had the same appearance, to judge from the samples to be found in the *Journal of Design* of 1851. It was first produced from the hair of the South American alpaca, and later from fine sheep wool. In its mid-nineteenth-century form it is difficult to identify, and being of wool, much may have been destroyed by insect depredations. Few of the great number of alpaca-covered parasols that were produced – 30,000 in 1849 alone[12] – seem to have survived, but the Patent Swiss parasol in Bath appears to be covered with alpaca.

Sangsters patented a seamless cover in 1855. Cover and lining were cut in one piece from a knitted fabric made on the warp frame machine, and a cord or fringe put around the edge to prevent stretching. Surviving examples have a printed border of flowers and motifs familiar from Paisley shawls, and are stretched over wire frames.

More elaborate, and consequently more expensive, parasols had covers of plain or *chiné* silk, with bands of brocading often checked or of floral designs, bunches of flowers in cut and uncut velvet, or any combination of these. Flounces, often with a pinked edge, appeared on parasols in the mid-1850s; one illustrated in the *Ladies' Cabinet* for May 1856, was 'of blue shaded silk bordered with a deep flounce, pinked at the edges. The handle is ivory cut in facets.' Although dresses with flounces woven *à disposition* had appeared in the early 1850s, they became particularly popular after 1856, and many parasols to the end of the decade have two or more frills. *Punch* lampooned this in a cartoon published on 13 November 1858, entitled 'A Neat Thing in Parasols': a lady in a flounced skirt holds a two-flounced parasol, with the ferrule forming the upper half of a female figure. Also in 1858, very small parasols called 'telegram' parasols appeared. Such a one is seen in the picture *A*

Summer's Day in Hyde Park by John Ritchie (1858). It cannot be more than ten inches in diameter and can have afforded very little protection from the sun. One of the few patents relating to covers was granted to M. Meyers in November 1858. The patent drawings show a two-tier cover with pinked scalloped edges, the lower tier curved between the rib tips, and a bow falling over the top tier. It was intended to be made in any fabric except silk. A parasol of similar appearance can be seen in the picture *Work* painted between 1852 and 1865 by Ford Madox Brown. Ribbons and bows appeared tied to the ferrule or anchored beneath it from the mid-1850s onwards, and applied decoration of various types continued into the 1860s.

According to the *Englishwoman's Domestic Magazine* for March 1862, the trousseau of a middle-class bride (income £400 to £600 per annum) should include one umbrella and two parasols. One of the latter would have

32   To Brighton and back for 3/6d., *signed and dated Charles Rossiter, 1859. The older woman carries a parasol of the plainer type of the 1840s, the cover cut in curves between the ribs; the young man is holding his girlfriend's carriage parasol. It might be made entirely of ivory, but is more likely to be white-painted wood with a small bone hook handle, typical of the cheaper parasols of the decade.*

been quite elaborate, the other a plainer walking parasol. Both would probably have had wire frames with white or coloured ball rib tips (a provisional patent in 1862 covers handles and rib tips of 'china, vitrified enamels or hard cement'). The walking parasol probably would have had a thin cane stick with a small hook, and from 1862 and 1867 might have been pagoda-shaped. ('They are stylish looking and to be quite in character with the pagoda shape, are seldom

33 *Fashion plate, June 1863, from the* Englishwoman's Domestic Magazine. *The trimmings of the light-coloured dress and the bonnet ribbons are magenta; the parasol is of the same colour covered with black lace.*

smaller than those of the earlier period. Covers were often in various shades of brown, nutmeg, cinnamon and 'the favourite Russian leather colour',[14] or in small checks and discreet patterns with or without satin borders. They accorded well with the plain or restrained patterned dress silks.

However, 'for occasions when a full dress parasol is required nothing is so suitable and *distingué* as black or white lace, made up over a bright coloured or white parasol'.[15] Although Irish guipure lace covers were shown at the Great Exhibition, it was only after 1858 that the lace parasol cover became really fashionable. In 1858 the *New Belle Assemblée* illustrated a grey parasol covered with Chantilly lace, and commented that lace was to be found on everything, 'from parasols to boots, lacemakers' cushions are again in request and hundreds of poor women and young girls employed in weaving the exquisite fabric'. In addition to black Chantilly lace and its imitations made on the Pusher and Leavers machines,

other laces such as Bedfordshire Maltese, Honiton, Brussels and Carrickmacross are to be found on parasols. Some covers were detachable and survive alone; some parasols with richly decorated handles have plain covers which were probably intended to have lace bought or made for them. In 1859 Mlle Riego de la Branchardière advertised patterns in point, Italian and Roman laces suitable for parasols and illustrated a cover in *The Lace Tatting Book* of 1866. The women's magazines carried patterns for either entire covers or decorative trimmings. Some suggested adapting

---

34 'Beatrice' parasol, c. 1868, probably named after Queen Victoria's youngest daughter: carved ivory handle set with coloured glass, silk cover in the square shape with truncated corners mentioned in F. Sangster's patent 598 of 1868. The fringe is tied into bunches, a feature on parasols of the later 1860s and early 1870s.

5 Parasols 1830–70. *Clockwise:* mother-of-pearl hook and ferrule, wood stick, blue satin woven with white silk bands, short woven fringe, 1845–55; length 30 inches, rib length 12½ inches, diameter open 22 inches. Wood handle, metal frame with enamelled rib tips, shot brown-and-black silk cover, on inside cap 'Superior Machine Made,' 1865–70; length 30½ inches, rib length 18½ inches, diameter open 30 inches. Carved ivory handle and ferrule, whalebone ribs with ivory tips, green silk cover opening to pagoda shape, ivory ring closure, 1830–40; length 38 inches, rib length 23 inches, diameter when open 34 inches. Cane handle, metal frame with enamelled rib tips, shot purple-and-black silk cover; on inside cap 'Best, Entered at Stationers Hall', similar to I. A. Boss's printed cap of 1862, 1860–70; length 29½ inches, rib length 18½ inches, diameter when open 29½ inches. Carved wood handle, cane ribs, bone ring, puce moiré cover with satin bands, sewn-on long fringe, 1850–60; length 29 inches, rib length 11½ inches, diameter when open 20 inches. Cane handle, metal frame with enamelled rib tips, brown silk cover with matching lining, 1860–70; length 28½ inches, rib length 13½ inches, diameter open 23 inches.

6 Parasol and *en-tout-cas. Left to right:* parasol with twisted cane handle, marked 'Regd. design 173511' (1891); curved gilt ribs (J. Allcock's patent 20,454 of 1894); shot pink-and-green silk cover; *c.* 1895. The pompoms on the handle were a French feature introduced in the 1880s. *En-tout cas* with tortoiseshell hook handle, brown ottoman silk cover. Mark: 'Brigg & Sons, London'. 1900–1915. *En-tout-cas* with painted cane L-shaped handle, gilt rib tips, blue silk cover with matching case. 1900–1910. *En-tout-cas* with bone handle carved with the lion of St Mark, Venice. Scored wood, brown silk cover on sixteen ribs, composition rib tips. Frame marked 'G.F.R.'. 1920–24.

7 Three Belgian parasols, mid-1920s. *Left:* horn handle carved as an owl, twelve-rib paragon-type frame, silk cover with edge turned over and frilled. *Centre:* ivory-ribbed cap to stout wood handle, wood stick, twelve-rib paragon-type frame. The cover forms a flower, the petals of white picot-edged georgette. *Right:* thick pistol-butt handle; wood stick; sixteen-rib paragon-type frame, opens flat. Imitation horn rib tips and one-piece tussore cover printed with Aztec-type pattern.

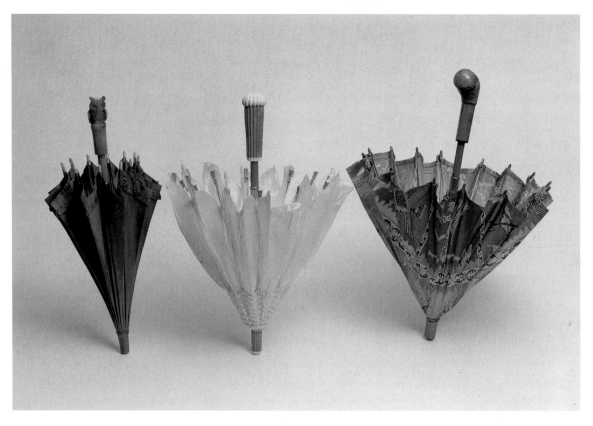

the thrifty hint of sewing black Maltese lace over a soiled light-coloured parasol. Fringe is not seen, except 'on one of those very dainty little articles trimmed with lace, and which are more for ornament than use'.[16] Perhaps the latter category would also include the marabou-feather-trimmed parasols popular in 1863 (and again in 1870). They were duchesse parasols, described as 'only a little larger than the *ombrelles marquises*',[17] and had been patronized by the Empress Eugénie, wife of Napoleon III, an elegant woman whose rank and taste made her a fashion leader. In September 1863 the *Englishwoman's Domestic Magazine* illustrates a dress of *solferino*-coloured silk, brocaded in black, and a feather parasol matching the dress. Aniline dyes (of which solferino was one) were discovered in the waste products of coal tar in 1856, but only became commercially available after 1859. Many of the flamboyant colours of the period,

patterns for round antimacassars or cushions. In June 1864 the *Englishwoman's Domestic Magazine* published a supplement with at least four designs for parasol covers; one for brown silk trimmed with imitation plaid of black lace applied over coloured silks, another for lilac embroidered with a band of flowers in red and green with black and yellow stars above, and a third for bead-trimmed lace. The same magazine in June 1862 included

36 Engraving from the magazine, the Girl of the Period, July 1869. Nearly all the girls in the magazine would have considered themselves fashionable; others would have called them 'fast'.

particularly the quickly fading purples, mauves and magentas were from aniline dyes.

The late 1860s was a period of indecision and experiment in female dress, as the crinoline reached the end of its long reign and the skirt hovered with or without various substructures until it settled on the bustle. This period stimulated fresh ideas for the parasol. Handles were thicker and many were club-shaped; covers were of odd designs. In 1867 H. Ellis of Bishop, Ellis & Co. had patented parasols with straight ribs and gores which opened to a flat or slightly conical shape. One, marked: 'B.E. & Co. Patent Parasol', is in Birmingham Museum; it has a blue silk cover and is probably *c.* 1870. In 1868 Francis Sangster was granted provisional patent No. 598, for parasols with stretchers of unequal length to create a ridge-and-furrow effect, or with unequally spaced ribs 'to form a parasol of approximately square form, but with truncated corners', or, by causing the runner to slide nearly to the top notch, 'to make a flat topped parasol, preferably covered with elastic fabric'. Although flat-topped or shallowly conical parasols, often fringed, are seen at this time (one with sixteen ribs and alternate brown and white gores is in the Gallery of English Costume, Manchester), only one named parasol can be definitely associated with either of these patents, and that is the 'Beatrice' parasol. One in Bath has 'Sangsters, The Beatrice Patent 598' on the runner. Some Beatrice parasols had covers shaped as a four-leafed clover. Truly square parasols appeared in 1869. They have only four ribs and are crudely made. They were presumably a fashion of the moment. Other strange shapes probably also belong to the end of the 1860s. Twelve-rib, flat-opening models with elaborately fringed moiré covers have been noted. A six-rib parasol in Bath with its long carved wooden handle and heavy cover of bead weaving probably belongs to this era too.

Most of the parasols of the early 1870s are in the same elaborate tradition as those of the previous two decades. Handles, however, became much stouter, often shaped like an onion or the thick end of a billiard cue, and carved with entwined foliage, or as a rigid chain. Many are short and thick. A feature was often made of ferrules. Loose or rigid rings, or knobs carved with leaves, are quite common. T-shaped ferrules are mentioned in the *Englishwoman's Domestic Magazine* of April 1870, and anchor-shaped ones are also known. Button shapes appeared in 1873, and from 1874 some ferrules had metal chains. More expensive parasols had the ferrule carved to match the handle. A charming model in Bath has both ends of ivory carved as the head of a peasant woman. The handle is telescopic, so that it can be short or long; the cover is black silk with a large bow of ribbon.

Covers are either the shallow shapes – cone, dome

and pagoda, continuing the line of the late 1860s – or a small deep dome. Unbleached silk, lawn and cambric appeared for cheaper parasols, and coloured linings were popular, particularly under the black covers which became fashionable in 1873. Lace trimmings at the edge and around the ferrule were often coarse machine-made lace or yak (handmade woollen lace), but in 1870 there was a revival of the fashion for Chantilly lace over white silk. The folding carriage parasol was on its way out; in J. & H. Tracy's patent of 1869 the hinge was replaced by a chain and the hinge cover by a bayonet fitting under a small band (sometimes marked Patent), so unobtrusive that its purpose is often not realized. The place of the long folding stick was taken by the short, thick, almost stubby handle for which there was a vogue on both sides of the Atlantic in 1873.

The opposite extreme, the long walking stick or staff parasol, had reappeared in 1870. The *Englishwoman's Domestic Magazine* in July 1870 described the 'Alpine costume of white serge and dark blue velvet, Tyrolese

37   Parasol, c. 1870. Ivory handle, plated metal stick, cast oval ring at ferrule end, cover of white marabou feathers shading to lilac at the edge, and white silk lining.

hat' and 'the long walking stick for climbing mountains, with a sunshade of unbleached foulard at the top'. Elsewhere, with a little hook and a brass ferrule, it appears as much a conscious revival of a hundred years earlier as the looped-up skirts and postillion jacket bodices were of Louis XV and Louis XVI fashions. Others had round or oval knobs, button tops, or fanciful shapes in composition or early plastic such as Parkesine, above ivory or wood turned to resemble bamboo, while others had billiard-cue ends, but all were long enough to be gripped easily. The sticks were long and thin. The cover was similar to other parasols and, like them, often of dark colours – maroon, black or burgundy in particular – trimmed with jet braid or fringe, lace, or flounces with pinked, scalloped edges. For those who could afford it, the parasol matched the dress in colour, fabric and trimmings. The staff parasol continued in fashion to 1879, but few exist in museum collections.

Similar to this type was the parasol with a handle at both ends, the one at the ferrule being smaller, so that it could always be carried with the ribs downwards. This was a style which continued into the 1880s.

UMBRELLAS

In spite of improvements to top notches and thinner ribs, the umbrella of the 1830s was still a bulky object, far removed in elegance from its rival, the cane. With the year 1840 came metal ribs and the chance to make a slimmer umbrella.

Although there had been experiments with metal ribs before, the first successful ones seem to have been those patented by Henry Holland of Birmingham in 1840. They were of steel tube, and made an umbrella that was both

38   Staff parasol, 1870–80. Ivory button top with gilt metal shield and the initials H.G., crown socket, rosewood stick with brass cap. The cover is of tussore silk trimmed with frills and machine lace, brown silk bow and lining. A parasol fashionable in its length, material and trimmings.

39   Parasol, 1870–80; ivory handle carved as a girl in classical costume picking roses, handmade needle lace (Brussels point de gaze) cover over lilac silk. An example of the truly expensive parasols of the period.

strong and light in weight. Similarly, even though solid steel ribs existed before 1848, by offering a rib, git and tip all in one, Samuel Fox persuaded umbrella makers to use his patent solid ribs. The secret of both lay in the tempering which gave the steel strength enough to spring frequently in and out of a curve, without distortion. In 1852 Fox patented a U-section rib and stretcher which sold with special furniture under the trade name 'Paragon' and was hugely successful. It enabled the ribs to come closer to the stick, thus making a slenderer article. Hardly modified, it is still produced today.

Few surviving umbrellas can be positively dated to

40   Umbrellas. Left to right: 1840–50: thick bamboo handle, thin black-japanned stick, rectangular metal ribs, green silk cover edged with blue-and-pink band. This belonged to the first Duke of Wellington (1769– 1852). Length 35¼ inches; rib length 27¾ inches. 1821–32: antler handle on cane stem, wood stick, brass spike, eight cane ribs with brass tips, shot green silk cover, and runner marked 'Hobday, Francis & Co. Royal Letters Patent'. Length 38½ inches. 1860–65: ivory or bone handle marked 'F. Lindner, Albion Road, Holloway' (owner), cane stick, and eight Paragon-type ribs with white tips. Brown cover, possibly alpaca. Marked 'Sangsters' on central reinforcement. Length 36¾ inches; rib length 27¾ inches. 1820–30: bone knob on painted wood stem, thick beech stick, 5¾-inch long runner, nine whalebone ribs, brass tips and spike, green-and-blue shot silk cover banded at the edge with pink. Length 38½ inches; distance between top of handle and rib tips 5¾ inches.

the 1840s and 1850s. There are, however, two umbrellas in the Museum of London which have metal frames and seem to belong to this era, although tradition places them earlier. One, which has a short straight wooden handle with a gilt metal cap, rectangular-section ribs and a pink silk cover banded at the edge, is said to have belonged to George IV (died 1830). If this is so (and there is nothing on the umbrella itself to prove royal ownership), then it is a very early example of metal ribs, and more likely to be French than English. The other has a short thick handle of bamboo, a very thin black-japanned metal stick, thick spike, and rectangular-section ribs. The cover is green silk with blue and pink bands at the edge. It is said to have belonged to the first Duke of Wellington, and to date from the early years of the century. As the Duke did not die until 1852, it is perhaps more likely to date from the 1840s, especially as it has the rather ungainly appearance, when open, of an experimental model. (See fig. 40.)

Judging from *Punch* and other sources, the most popular handles seem to have been the crutch, the small hook and the natural L-shaped branches of various trees. In 1856, a letter to *Punch* made an impassioned plea for knob handles, since hooks caught in the folds of dresses and tore them. In the 1850s the pistol-butt shape became popular. All, presumably, were made both in wood and ivory with brass, gilt metal or silver bands. Antler and horn handles were still common. Handles carved as human heads, as in the 1830s, were probably still popular. A number are humorously depicted on the title page of *Memoirs of an Umbrella* by G. Herbert Rodwell (1845), together with handles carved as birds' heads, and as a human hand grasping a bar. Covers seem to be

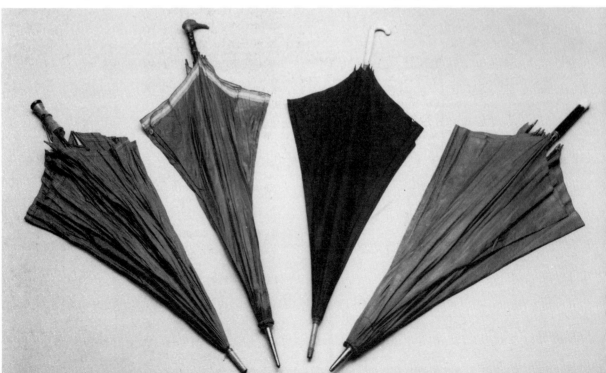

shallow or deep-domed. Silk, mainly green and brown, banded at the edge, was used both on the new metal frames and on the cheaper cane and whalebone frames which continued to be made. An example in the Victoria & Albert Museum has a stained ivory bar handle, cane grip, nine whalebone ribs with bone tips, a brass-tipped long ferrule and open cap, and a brown silk cover with cream banding at the edge. Similar frames covered with cotton, 'gamps', were still seen, but were more and more objects of derision – especially in *Punch*.

As with parasols, alpaca was increasingly used from 1848 onwards as a cheaper alternative to silk. Alpaca-covered umbrellas could be purchased from Sangsters for 10s. 6d. each in 1850.[18] Advertisements give some idea of the comparative prices of umbrellas; for instance, in January 1853 John Cheek, Manufacturer, Golden Perch, 132 Oxford Street, London, advertised, 'The new patent Umbrella, the lightest and strongest, covered with Cheek's pure Italian silk, is the best; constructed under Mr Cheek's immediate inspection, and warranted. Silk 6s. to 23s., alpacas 7s. to 15s., gingham 2s. to 8s., Carriage umbrellas 3s. 6d. to 31s. 6d.' John Cheek's name does not appear in the list of patentees for the years previous, and the 'new patent umbrella' might be the new Fox Paragon frame of 1852. Again, as with parasols, alpaca-covered umbrellas are difficult to identify. One possible candidate is in the Museum of London (see fig. 40); it probably dates from between 1860 and 1865.

Umbrella makers did not carry large stocks in terms of quantity, but did offer a wide range of types and styles. The stock book of James Smith & Co. for 1862 lists six qualities in solid metal, and Paragon frames in five rib lengths, from 21½ inches to 27½ inches. Covered in silk, the price varied from 7s. 6d. to 14s. for 21½-inch solid frames, 9s. to 15s. 6d. for Paragon frames, 13s. to 21s. for 27½-inch solid frames, 14s. to 23s. for Paragon. The same covered with alpaca varied from 4s. to 9s. for 21½-inch, 7s. 6d. to 12s. for 27½-inch solid frames. Paragon frames cost up to 2s. each extra. Colours were either green or brown, silk covers for ladies' umbrellas had a border, and best-quality alpaca had a wide border of three stripes. In the list of umbrellas, pimento handles and silver buckles are mentioned (the latter were probably silver bands imitating buckled straps), but the stock also included 40 bamboo canes with ivory handles at 2s. each, 138 natural hook bamboos at 9s. per dozen, oaks at 4s. 6d., and firs at 6s. These were presumably ready for putting on to wood or metal sticks. Unfortunately, few umbrellas with gold or silver bands of this period can be positively dated from hallmarks, as precious metal articles weighing under five pennyweights troy were exempt from hallmarking.

41   Umbrella, c. 1850; ivory button top carved with fox's mask, japanned brass telescopic tube stick, folding ribs, bottle-green silk twill cover, ivory ferrule cap (not shown), and ivory ring closure, marked 'Pittar Patentee'; this umbrella accords very closely with S.J. Pittar's Patent No. 13,223 of 1850.

After 1852 the fashionable umbrella became so much slimmer, that it was the subject of a number of *Punch* cartoons in the mid-1850s. It reflected the change in men's outward appearance, from the waisted style padded at the chest and hips to the thin vertical line with the tall ('stove pipe') hat on top. Some umbrellas, 'long and light as a sunbeam',[19] especially those with solid frames, might well have been mistaken for parasols, or their plainer relation, the *en-tout-cas*. What appears to be an *en-tout-cas* in Bath could also be an umbrella of *c.* 1860–65. It is not quite of walking length, and the short distance between the rib tips and the top of the handle is commonly found on umbrellas to past the half-century. Most umbrellas of the 1850s were probably thicker than this. Some idea of their appearance can be gauged from *The Last of England*, painted by Ford Madox Brown between 1852 and 1855: two emigrants gaze out to sea, the woman partly sheltered under a large puce umbrella. The painting is so meticulous that the spring and metal ribs are clearly visible; unfortunately the handle is hidden from view. An umbrella as thin as a walking stick and described as 'the most compact and lightest of any yet manufactured'[20] was patented by Captain Francis Fowke and shown at the International Exhibition of 1862. In February 1873, Samuel Fox was advertising a curved rib which lay tighter to the stick; they were available from April onwards at 3*d.* extra per dozen sets.

Although most umbrellas were rather plain, utilitarian articles, finer models were made, presumably more for show than use. One in Derby Museum probably dates from between 1865 and 1875 (see fig. 43).

Women's umbrellas from the 1840s onwards are difficult to identify. Like those of the 1820s and 1830s, they were probably indistinguishable from men's, except that they were smaller and lighter. Costume of the period did not lend itself to much walking in conditions where an umbrella would be necessary. Those who could afford to either owned carriages or hired them. Those that could not probably used a cotton-covered 'gamp'. However, John Cheek did advertise in 1854, 'Ladies' Brown Silk Umbrella, 7s.; the French myrtle and Napoleon blue 13s., and the London Smoke, of pure Italian silk 19s.', and 'The

---

42 Small by degrees, and beautifully less, *Punch cartoon, 22 December 1855, satirizing the slender umbrella of the 'swell'. Although Paragon frames did enable a smaller umbrella to be made, they were never this thin!*

SMALL BY DEGREES, AND BEAUTIFULLY LESS.

Shopman. "Oh, I beg your Pardon, Sir—but the Lady left her Parasole on the Counter!"
Swell. "Haw! Ya—as—No! That is, it's my Umbrellaw. Thanks! By Jove! Haw!"

New Light Umbrella, so light and strong it excels every other kind – Ladies' size 11s. to 21s., according to quality of silk and style of handle.'

It is probable that the various collapsible or telescopic umbrellas invented in this period were intended for women's use. One of the earliest to survive dates from about 1850 and is in the Museum of Costume, Bath. It is marked 'Pittar, Patentee', and closely resembles the drawings in Samuel John Pittar's patent, No. 13,223, of 1850. It is also unusual in that the runner is pushed upwards to close the umbrella. Another, more than twenty years later in date, is in the Victoria & Albert Museum. It, too, has folding ribs and a telescopic stick, and is covered in dark-green silk twill. The handle is a cane hook and the inside cap is printed: 'Patent, Lake & Co., 16 Regent Street, London W.' It can be related to patent 975, granted to W.R. Lake in 1875.

Another women's umbrella which appeared in 1862 but was particularly fashionable in the early 1870s, does not seem to have had a specific name. It is a small umbrella attached to a waist belt. In 1872 the *Queen* magazine suggested in answer to a query about travelling dress that a leather belt tipped with silver be worn: 'They are costly but the metal is pure and will not tarnish even with sea air, and chatelaines can be attached or separate hooks for a smelling bottle, fan or umbrella, both very useful for travelling.' In October 1872 the *Queen* reported among Parisian fashions, 'The newest belts are made of either black or maroon velvet, ornamented with Renaissance agrafes [hooks], made of chased silver, and lined with either pink or blue silk . . . The small umbrellas suspended from the belts are invariably black, with ebony handles encrusted with silver.' A chatelaine bag was always sold with it. An umbrella of white silk lined with pink, and a parasol of Chinese embroidery, both with ivory handles and chased silver mounts, were among the appendages to be attached to a 'Norwegian Belt' which Mr Thornhill of Bond Street, London made for a lady customer in the same year. In 1874 it was suggested that a sunshade or *en-tout-cas* be clipped to the belt. These umbrellas and the belts frequently appear in the fashion plates of the period, but none could be identified as such in any of the museum collections examined, though a few umbrellas had a silver ring on the handle to which, as was suggested 'a small chain is fastened, which can be put over the arm or hooked on to an agrafe at the waist'.[21]

THE *EN-TOUT-CAS*

Midway between the parasol and the umbrella is the *en-tout-cas*. Smaller than the umbrella, plainer than the parasol, it was an English invention given a French name.

43 Umbrella, 1865–75. Ivory handle carved as an eagle attacking a snake on a tree trunk, cane stick, Paragon frame, hand-stitched puce silk twill cover with checked band at edge. Marked on inside cap 'Fox's Paragon Patent'; 'Paragon' on a tablet on one stretcher.

Parasols which also fulfilled the functions of umbrellas had been known as early as Robinson Crusoe's umbrella of 1719, and some of the plain, dark parasols of the 1820s also served as umbrellas. But it was not until the early 1860s that the *en-tout-cas* is described as a new phenomenon. In July 1861 the *Englishwoman's Domestic Magazine* reported, 'The sunshades and *ombrelles* – or as the French call them, *Les en-tout-cas* – which are made large enough to serve as an umbrella as well as a parasol, are also extremely useful for travelling.' In 1862 they are described as being of 'brown, drab or dark green for morning or walking costume and white or some delicate shade for more dressy toilets'. A parasol with a thin cane stick, small hook handle and a dark-green silk cover much larger than usual, in Bath, might

44 From the Milliner, Dressmaker and Warehouseman's Gazette, *July 1874. The waist belts are steel-trimmed leather with steel chains for the sunshades; below, the central staff parasol is a 'Louis XV ombrelle' edged with feathers, the two to the left are* en-tout-cas, *one of spotted foulard, the other of brown silk, and the two on the right are respectively a 'Marquise ombrelle' with ivory handle and cover in two colours, and a 'Trianon ombrelle' edged with striped foulard. Confusion of types and terms is typical of the 1870s.*

be an early *en-tout-cas*, or an umbrella – the distinction between a plain parasol, an *en-tout-cas* and an umbrella is not obvious.

The *en-tout-cas* gained in popularity as women began to enjoy a more active outdoor life. Early signs of emancipation had been expressed by Mrs Amelia Bloomer in America in 1851, but her short skirt and full trousers gathered at the ankle had been ridiculed into extinction. The speedy adoption of the lightweight steel crinoline freed the legs from clinging petticoats. In Britain Queen Victoria tramped the Scottish hillsides wearing thick-soled Balmoral boots, and in 1868 published *Leaves from the Journal of Our Life in the Highlands*. In France the Empress Eugénie popularized a shorter skirt, said to have been designed by the couturier Worth to show off her slender feet. Thomas Cook, who had started his travel company with a short train excursion from Leicester to Loughborough in 1841, organized trips to Europe in the 1860s, and by the 1870s, as photographs show, women as well as men were climbing in the Alps. Not only for travelling, but for walking too, the dual purpose *en-tout-cas* was ideal.

In 1873 the *Queen* announced that '*En-tout-cas* are now taking the place of umbrellas.' They were covered with twilled silk or shot Venetian silk in black and blue or purple. The short, stout handle was malacca or bamboo with knobs of ivory, mounted in 'oxydized silver-gilt' with a chain to clip to the chatelaine. The rib length was 18 inches. As with the parasol, the *en-tout-cas* was supposed to match the dress in colour.

British weather being perpetually doubtful, the *en-tout-cas* was a useful compromise, and its popularity continued well into the next century.

PARASOL-WHIPS

Another form of parasol from this period was the parasol-whip: a parasol mounted halfway up the shaft of a driving whip. M. Cazal, the French umbrella maker, mentioned a 'sunshade whip' in his book *Umbrellas, Parasols and Walkingsticks* (1844). John Leech, in a cartoon in *Punch* in November 1858, showed a fringed example in the hands of a dashing belle in a low-slung, basket-bodied park phaeton drawn by a pony. The same phaeton and whip appeared in the Leech illustration 'Rosa at Mayfield', in R.S. Surtees's novel *Plain or Ringlets* (1860).

In *Good Wives* (American title *Little Women, part II*), Louisa Alcott described the scene on the Promenade des Anglais, Nice, in the middle of the 1860s, 'the low basket barouches in which ladies drive themselves, with a pair of dashing ponies, gay nets to keep their voluminous flounces from overflowing the diminutive

vehicles'. Amy March, in one of these carriages, preferred to drive, 'for her parasol-whip and blue reins over the white ponies' backs, afforded her infinite satisfaction'.

A parasol-whip with a holly shaft and long tapering handle is in the Cheltenham Museum. The handle has an ivory cap and band, and the parasol a solid metal frame covered with black silk frilled at the edge, and lined with white silk. It dates probably from between 1850 and 1870. Another, at the Gallery of English Costume, Manchester, also has a solid metal frame covered in brown-and-black shot silk with a pinked frill at the edge; the lining is also pinked. The long ivory handle is carved with crossing cords with tassels. The mounts are silver, hallmarked in Birmingham in 1870.

The parasol-whip seems to have died out with the 1870s. It was probably not all that common, as women drivers, even in such feminine carriages, were considered 'fast', while the 'strong minded woman' of the era would not have approved of such a frivolous article.

45 *Parasol-whip, 1870: painted wood stick, carved* ▷
ivory handle, silver cap and band, solid metal ribs with
black-and-brown silk cover.

5

1875-1920

Although there was no resemblance, except in restriction, between the sheathlike successor to the bustle dress, and the dresses of the 1840s, there was, in the late 1870s, a revival of the parasol styles of the 1840s.

In 1877 the marquise returned as the 'parasolette' or 'drop parasol', in dark silk trimmed with ribbon loops of two contrasting colours, a stick of natural cherry wood, and gold-painted ribs. (This was virtually the first time that attention had been drawn to the ribs, although Samuel Fox had offered coloured ribs as early as 1852.) The pagoda reappeared in *La Mode Illustrée* in May 1877 as 'une ombrelle Chinoise' and, confusingly, as 'the Japanese parasol', embroidered and trimmed with 'Spanish' lace, in the *Queen* of March 1879. 'As bows of ribbon would hide the pagoda top, they are relegated to the side.'[1] Handles were of light thistlewood decorated with ribbon bows. Some covers had gores cut in a curve at the edge, a revival, again, of a style of the 1840s and 1850s. The trimming was usually lace, or fringe, either crimped, or of the corrugated black braid known as 'copeau', much used on mantles. The revived pagoda had a short life; the flat pagoda was more typical of the 1880s.

A revival of an even older style appeared at the end of the 1870s: the flat parasol with numerous ribs. Again there was a confusion of terms. Unnamed in the *Milliner and Dressmaker* for July 1879, it was 'Chinese' in *Cassells' Family Magazine* for May 1880, and 'Japanese' in the same publication in August. 'The cover is black satin and the lining is satin to match the trimmings of the dress worn at the time. The frame is made with sixteen ribs, and these are visible, the lining being beneath them.'[2] A similar parasol is in the Museum of Costume and Textiles, Nottingham, but it has a rustic wood handle instead of 'the rooting portion of a large reed (*Arundo clonax*) golden yellow in colour and marked with ringlike ridges of dark brown'.[3] On both parasols the cover is held closed by another revival, a ring (of cord or covered metal) on a cord attached to the spike, but 'it is certainly ugly, wears out the silk, and is quite useless, as the usual mode of fastening is also there'.[4]

The still-fashionable dome was, by 1880, 'preposterously large; many have resembled small tents'.[5] It, too, often had gores curved at the base. Huge cream or black satin parasols with rustic handles and 'Spanish' lace or crêpe lisse trimming are typically 1880s. In June 1883, however, the *Girl's Own Paper* announced the arrival of colour: 'We have got rid of the hues of decaying vegetables, and have launched out into what are known as "fruit tints", which are bright and peculiar.' Examples were orange, apricot, and crushed strawberry. Although parasols, and other accessories, ideally matched the dress, few can be recognized in these colours, or in the Turkey red, bright claret and yellow, which were allegedly so popular. Occasionally, however, brightly coloured linings can be seen in parasols of black satin.

Covers were often embroidered, by machine in 'ombré' silks or by hand. Periodicals gave patterns: of crimson and yellow roses on a blue ribbon in 1880, or swallows in natural colours or 'merely outlined in gold thread',[6] in Japanese style, in 1889. Flowers and flowerheads, as in 1881, were perennial favourites, and feathers appeared occasionally too; but a cover embroidered with peacock feathers in the *Queen* for May 1879 had been anticipated by *Punch* in April 1871. Techniques such as braiding and smocking found on children's and women's informal dress were also used; smocking for this purpose was patented in 1888.

In the era of amateur 'artistic' creativity, painting was another type of decoration. The landscapes and flowers found on the outside of the parasol in the early 1880s[7] were replaced by owls' heads, large spiders and beetles on the lining in 1883.[8] Some of the painting, notably butterflies on a cover in Derby Museum (fig. 46), and frogs on a lining in Cheltenham Museum, looks Japanese in style and technique. Printed linings are also found. Figures in eighteenth-century costume in scenes of harlequinade and blind-man's buff were printed by chromolithography on the cream cotton lining of a pink sateen parasol in the Museum of Costume, Bath.

Lace was still popular, both as a trimming and as a fabric. Small lace parasol covers of the late 1850s and 1860s were reused with muslin and lace on the larger

frames of the 1880s. Machine-made lace, the product of the Leavers machines of Nottingham, and the embroidering machines of Switzerland and Germany, was gathered in tiers on parasols from 1880 onwards. This was a popular fashion, as it could disguise a soiled cover or a cheap fabric. Parasol covers entirely of lace, with no linings, supported on cords between the ribs,

46   Parasol, 1880–85: white satin cover painted in the Japanese style with butterflies, chiffon frill, cane stick with porcelain handle.

47 *Parasol, 1885–90: black machine-made lace imitating Chantilly; black crêpe painted with a seated woman, ribbon bows and cherubs; tortoiseshell handle with applied putto and flowers; two-tone gold decoration; and covered frame. The decoration is asymmetrical on each gore.*

were fashionable in 1883.[9] They and the half-lace, half-fabric covers were considered 'the most nonsensical of all, for how can a transparent material like lace protect one from the sun?'[10] One such in Derby Museum is black lace and chiffon painted with a seated woman, cherubs and flowers (see fig. 47). Handmade lace was still greatly prized. One parasol, a wedding present in the early 1880s, was 'entirely covered with point lace on a pink ground, clouded with white gauze, having a jade handle with incrustations of precious stones up to its extreme point. A golden ring gemmed with emeralds and brilliants, attached to a gold chain, served as a clasp for this inestimable jewel.'[11] Silver or silver-gilt handles,

---

48 *Plainer parasols of the 1880s and 1890s.* Left: *black satin cover, piped and trimmed with 'Spanish' lace, chip-carved ebonized wood stick with a hook at either end, 1880–85. Length 34¼ inches; rib length 16 inches; diameter open 30 inches.* Centre: *black cotton twill cover printed with silver lines, tapering chip-carved ebonized wood handle, 1890–1910. Length 35½ inches; rib length 19½ inches; diameter open 33 inches.* Right: *black silk twill cover opening to deepish dome, band of openwork weaving near edge, carved ebonized wood crutch handle, 1890–1900. Length 35½ inches; diameter open 32½ inches.*

49 *Photograph, dated 9 May 1885; the umbrella (which might be an* en-tout-cas) *has the typical looped handle of the 1880s.*

possibly of French workmanship, set with gems, which are found on parasols covered with handmade lace, probably belong to the years around 1880.

The commonest handles of the 1880s were of wood, often ebonized, bent by steam into curves, crooks, narrow hooks, loops, knots and 'question marks'. Nearly all were of walking length, although 'the new lace-trimmed parasols are very bulky, and are now carried cuddled up like an infant on the arm, as they are really too large to carry otherwise'.[12] Some spikes were short and had no metal ferrule. More elaborate parasols had richer handles, in 1879 carved pugs', pheasants' or pigeons' heads, or a swan, its neck curved to form a hook;[13] in 1882 balls of lapis lazuli and French and German porcelain in eighteenth-century style.[14] In 1884, 'pistol butt ends of curious and antique styles. The hilts of rapiers of all dates are represented, and bejewelled dagger handles. Specimens of carving in ancient and much-discoloured ivory are very popular – porcelain tops of huge size, serpents, ducks, owls, swans and dogs' heads carved in wood'.[15] Pink celluloid and Russian-

leather-covered handles were new in 1885, together with apples, pears and oranges – 'in fact all kinds of vegetables except potatoes'.[16] Handles as large as billiard balls were noted in 1888, and snakeskin for covering in 1895.[17] Knob handles, often with long sockets, ring handles from 1883 onwards, and long tapering handles from the late 1880s, are all popular styles which continue beyond the 1890s.

The 1880s saw the reappearance and disappearance of the bustle. Elaborately draped skirts gave place only slowly to the plainer styles of the 1890s. Trimmings were eccentric, inspired by or exploiting the natural world. Birds and insects – as well as flowers and leaves, both real and imitation – trimmed dresses and accessories including parasols; insects and monkeys were carved on handles in 1888.[18] Straw-covered parasols, also found in the 1870s, matched straw fans and hats at Trouville in 1882.[19] Large dog-head handles enlivened impractical velvet parasols in 1883.[20] Ostrich feathers trimmed satin covers in 1883 and 1885. Flowers were also popular, both cultivated and wild; 'grasses, oats and wheat, thistles and dandelions' in 1884, with climbing lilac and wisteria for borders.[21] L. Rogers patented a flower-shaped cover in 1887 and in 1888 Madame Mirabeau presented the 'Rose' parasol to the Princess of Wales as a silver-wedding gift. It was white muslin over pink silk, edged with Brussels lace, with a large blush rose at the top.[22] 1888 was the year for flower parasols: sunflowers, 'waterlilies, primroses, fuchsias and snowdrops have been utilised, sometimes in bands and fringes, simply serving as trimmings on silk, lace, velvet and muslin . . . and sometimes the flower constitutes the parasol'.[23] The Floriform of the 1850s revived! Sadly, these creations seem to have perished, along with the boas of real red roses and the parasol trimmings of freshly picked daisies.

There were eccentric shapes of cover, too. In 1885 it was fashionable to place two handkerchiefs or squares of material one across the other to make an eight-pointed star. The edges might be trimmed with lace, and though unlined, 'a fall of lace is sometimes added inside which must be a dreadful nuisance to the holder'.[24] Other shapes in 1887 were polygonal: triangles, pentagons, hexagons and octagons.[25]

50 *Handle, 1887–90, set with keyless fob watch in the top, silver-plated casing.*

Cheaper and simpler sunshades for morning and everyday use existed. They had plain hook or 'rustic' handles and sometimes solid wire frames. They were made in 'plain red, or cream lined with a colour, in cashmerienne mixtures, with borders, and of charming Pompadour cottons which would make a cotton costume very complete indeed'. Pompadour cottons printed with flowers are often bordered with black. Bordered linings, coloured under plain holland from 1879, or black with white, and white with black, are also seen. Tussore (unbleached) silk, printed or plain, was also popular. Towards the end of the decade both black and white moiré became fashionable for the plainer parasol, foreshadowing the simpler styles of the 1890s.

By 1894 'sunshades favour the umbrella type, simple and plain, with slender handles of natural form in either cherrywood, bramble or thorn'.[26] Ebony handles had 'small knobs painted with Watteau figures, or a group of tiny balls in chrysoprase'.[27] Black-striped white silk sprinkled with roses, black moiré with yellow lace insertion, black satin with radiating lines of insertion, shot or plain silk with borders of graduated stripes and *chiné* silks, were all popular. Sadly, much of the silk

around the turn of the century was weighted with tin salts and has split alarmingly, so that the charm of these parasols can no longer be appreciated.

The plainer parasols corresponded with the more tailored look that came with the passing of the bustle. Though skirts could be full, even threatening a return of the crinoline, they fitted at the waist and over the hips. Bodices were tight, too, but sleeves reached 1830s proportions between 1893 and 1897. This was the dress of the active woman, the New Woman, who achieved unchaperoned freedom on the new safety bicycle.

Like the frothy underwear hidden under the plain skirts, many plain parasols when opened revealed elaborate linings: 'Sunshades are like flowers, lined with waves of "ombré" chiffon, of the loveliest shades.'[28] A bridal parasol in 1896 was trimmed with white gauze frills inside, the stitching on the outside hidden by rows of sequins. The charm of these parasols lay in their impracticability: 'The real elegance of a sunshade should consist in a light mount and an original handle; this is more to the purpose than investing in frilled chiffon parasols, which look tumbled after they have been worn a couple of times.'[29] Nevertheless, these 'Geisha' parasols, as they were called, after the musical comedy, continued into the next decade.

Handles were various. Crutch handles in ebonized wood, chip-carved with flowers or Japanese ornament, were popular, but long tapering handles and ball knobs

52 Handles. Left to right: *1900–1910: enamelled silver made to represent a closed crocus; typical of the art nouveau flower handles at the turn of the century. 1906: rock-crystal knob set with sapphires, partridge cane stick. 1905–15: cut-glass ball, deep sterling silver band which unscrews to reveal a scent bottle. 1900–1910: celluloid monkey's head which has a lever to roll the eyes and stick out the tongue, cane stick stamped 'Brigg'. 1911: nephrite handle set with a ruby in a diamond circle which pulls out as the top of a pencil. 1908: quartz, enamel and silver gilt knob on sycamore stem; it has its own grey suede-covered box marked '23 Juin 1908', possibly a wedding or birthday present.*

were especially fashionable. The parasol presented to Queen Victoria 'by Her Majesty's oldest parliamentary subject', C.P. Villiers, on 20 June 1897, and carried by her in the Diamond Jubilee procession, has a gunmetal knob set with 'VRI' in diamonds. It was made by J.C. Vickery of Regent Street, London, famous for expensive gem-set knick-knacks. Two parasols made to celebrate the same jubilee are in the Victoria & Albert Museum and the Museum of London. Both have ball knobs, one gilt on a porcelain pillar with portraits of the Queen in 1837 and 1897; the other with a portrait of the young Queen and 'VR 1837'. The first has a white *glacé* cover woven with grey *chiné* flowers over a ruched chiffon lining; the other is plain black silk over ribs cased in silk, a feature of many expensive parasols from this period onwards.

The Jubilee year also saw a change in emphasis away from stiff dress fabrics towards softer, clinging materials, foreshadowing the look now associated with the Edwardians. Ethereal fabrics were popular, especially chiffon, which became the keyword for the next decade.

Edward VII was over fifty when he came to the throne, and his court had on the whole grown older with him. Both the King and Society favoured the woman of over forty. The fashions of the day favoured her too; the straight-fronted corset which pushed out the bust and hips looked best on a stouter figure, and the mature woman had the poise to wear large hats and clothes dripping with fussy trimmings. Now more than ever, these clothes expressed social status and a sizeable income. The most complicated had yards of invisible handwork, and parasols again became elaborate confections. Lace was popular – 'Every woman who can afford to . . . will have a real lace parasol mounted over

53   Parasol of 1900–1910 in cream silk warp-frame lace embroidered by machine in chain stitch with applied braid, painted porcelain handle, white-painted stick, silk-covered frame. Length 36½ inches; diameter open 32 inches.

chiffon'[30] – sometimes with painted gauze medallions set into the lace, sometimes sparkling with sequins and glass brilliants. The lace was often tape lace or machine-made lace, re-embroidered with ribbon. Colours were pastel, enlivened occasionally by a stronger tint: a bright-red poppy-shaped parasol in chiffon with an enamelled poppy-bud handle in 1899, and a red-and-white striped one in 1904. Shaded effects were popular: shaded blue chiffon over pale blue *chiné* silk in 1904 or worn with shaded ostrich feather boas or tulle ruffles in 1905. A parasol in the Museum of London, carried at a wedding in 1905, has a gilt button knob and a cover of *glacé* silk with satin bands shading from white to orange. The lining is ruched yellow silk with machine-embroidered frills. Shot effects, especially in chiffon, were also seen. A parasol of green silk 'lined with frill upon frill of accordion pleated shot green and black

54   Ascot, c. 1905: the most elaborate parasol in this typical view is to the right of centre; it has a wavy edge and appears to be trimmed with flowers. With the exception of the one on the left, probably a chiné-printed silk, all the others are either plain sunshades or light-coloured en-tout-cas.

chiffon' was carried with a silk afternoon dress 'trimmed with quaint ruchings of black satin', and a green-and-black straw hat decorated with ostrich feathers and cornflowers. The whole was considered 'the essence of chic simplicity'.[31] Black-and-white had not lost its appeal, and in 1905 a Chantilly lace parasol, lined with white chiffon, provided the finishing touch to a princess frock of Irish crochet over accordion pleated chiffon-voile. Truly, as one fashion writer commented in 1899, 'if we cannot

7002

Bodice 7019:
skirt 7015

Blouse 6954; skirt 7025

Bodice 6994: skirt 7009

DELIGHTFULLY novel in line and effect
is design 7002. Striking style features
are seen in the flare skirt and the jumper with
bretelles. For a woman of medium size there
will be required to reproduce the dress as illustrated two yards and seven-eighths of novelty
ratine forty-four inches wide for the skirt and
jumper, with two yards and one-eighth of or-
gandy thirty-six inches wide for the blouse, and
one yard and one quarter of edging to trim.

The dress consists of a three-piece flare skirt
in clearing length with soft fulness at the top of
the back. It may be made with or without the
inverted pleat and its lower edge measures in
the medium size about two yards without the
pleat and two yards and three-eighths with the
pleat. To the skirt is attached the jumper with
bretelles, and the separate blouse is made with
body in one with full-length or shorter sleeves
which are wide at the upper part. The collar
in stand-away effect is extremely attractive.

Design 7002 in seven sizes, thirty-two to forty-
four inches bust measure, and costs sixpence.

Dress 7002

7025   6994   7009   7015   7019   7002

manage to look beautiful with such a setting . . . we don't deserve to have such opportunities offered to us'.[32]

Handles complemented the covers. Tapering handles and ball knobs were still the most fashionable, the latter extending into all sorts of carved conceits. A catalogue dated 1897 at James Smith & Co. Ltd gives some idea of the variety in tortoiseshell handles. They range from carved heads – hares', dogs', babies' – to rings, crutches

---

◁ *55   From the* Delineator, *July 1914; the deep dome and the contrast of black and white were both fashionable at this period. The long handles complement the vertical line of the dresses.*

---

56   Men's umbrella handles. Left to right: *antler cross handle, silver band, wood stick, 1881. Ivory hook, gold band, partridge cane stem, 1889. The frame has the rib tips of c. 1910; an expensive handle has been reused on a more up-to-date frame. Imitation tortoiseshell crutch handle with copper-gilt bands, ebony stem; the lower band acts as a rib-tip cup, 1890–1910. Whangee hook with silver band, 1904. Lengths of handles: 5¼/6/6/6½ inches; lengths of umbrellas: 35¾/36¼/35/35½ inches.*

and ball knobs. Prices are given for plated (i.e. tortoiseshell veneer over a cheaper base), and solid. A hare's head, for instance, cost 7s. 5d. plated, 25s. solid. Close imitations were also available. Tortoiseshell handles with gold initials were fashionable in 1899, along with handles studded with imitation diamonds. Some handles were novelties, opening to reveal coins, cigarettes or pencils; some, in 1904, were 'abnormally long Pompadour handles, surmounted by a ball of pure, cut crystal', or crystal enclosing an enamelled flower or dog's head, the invention of J.C. Vickery. The more valuable handles had bayonet fittings so that they were removable. A quartz, enamel and silver-gilt handle at the Museum of Costume, Bath, has its own suede-covered box marked '23 Juin 1908', perhaps a birthday or wedding present. Detached Fabergé handles have later been made into paperknives and magnifying glasses. Parasols illustrated in a 1902 catalogue for les Grands Magasins Samaritaine, Paris, show a preponderance of ball knobs, with the occasional loop, dog's head or crutch, usually with a puff of chiffon, pompoms, ribbon bows or tassels tied to the stick. Covers range from embroidered or lace-bordered *silésienne* to accordion-pleated lace and moiré cut into points above ribbon frills. All are either black or cream. Parasols in a Sears Roebuck catalogue, also of 1902, are black or white with hook or L-shaped handles.

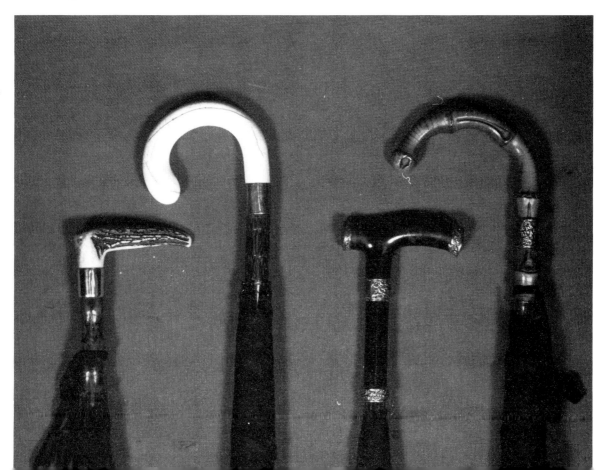

From about 1907, as dresses began to lose the froth associated with the early years of the century, anticipating the narrow skirts of the next decade, the parasol, too, became plainer. Trimmings were often no more than a couple of narrow frills or hemstitched tucks. Some parasols in 1908 were made entirely of chiffon, and lace, when used, was often applied flat as a border. After 1911, light covers with dark borders of satin, moiré or velvet were popular. Black velvet parasols, recorded in London in 1910, were lined with light silk and fringed in 1911; white velvet parasols were covered with black cobweb lace.[33] Linings were more interesting: hand-painted chiffon inside a cover of lace-edged surah in 1912, or silk printed with flowers.[34] Parasols were often kept closed by a cord round the rib tips, so that the lining was always visible.

The commonest shape was the dome, which became very deep between 1913 and 1918, supported on up to 16 ribs. In America 12 ribs were 'now regarded as standard for the higher grades',[35] though up to 24 could be used. In 1910 the pagoda returned, with part of the ribs flattened to make a mushroom shape. One of these in Bath has twelve gilt ribs, a lavender-banded navy-blue cover and an ebonized wood handle. The runner is marked 'Patent 14388', referring to J. Rose's patent of 1910. In 1911 this shape lost its central point, and, by special cutting of the cover, became the 'drop edge or lampshade'[36] parasol. The bell shape, which had the ends of ribs permanently curved in 1895, reappeared with the ends flattened to lie close to the stick. These new shapes were particularly popular in America.

Hook handles were becoming increasingly common, especially for plain sunshades, and in 1908 long 'Directoire' handles.[37] Some of these handles were provided with ribbon loops so that they could be 'slung over the shoulders in the same manner as a schoolboy carries his satchel'! Directoire handles usually taper like a billiard cue handle, or curve into a trumpet shape. From 1910 some are oval or octagonal in section. Many unscrew, 'which is a great convenience when travelling'.[38] Most are of wood, and often finished in a light-toned paint which flakes off easily. Ring handles revived in a new form in 1908: 'About the newest thing is the floral painted handle to slip over the hand and is embellished with carved leaves and flowers, the stalk forming the ring'[39]; the ordinary ring handle returned in 1911. Large button tops, known as 'table tops', also appeared in 1908. Carved handles were still popular, with birds and animals represented, either as a head or whole. In 1912 the *Ladies' Field* illustrated seven handles carved with dogs, all on trumpet-shaped bases of crystal, and mentioned mechanical handles – one being a cuckoo house with a bird on a spring – for plain

57 Left: *woman's umbrella: chased silver handle with a vinaigrette under a flap at the top, 1888, lock-rib frame, black silk twill cover. Right: man's umbrella; ivory handle, gilt band inscribed 'Presented to Mr. I. Uridge as a mark of esteem from a few members of the Bromley Cycling Club, Oct. 1896', rattan cane stick, black silk cover.* ▷

parasols. These handles were in composition or in the new plastics such as xylonite, bakelite or erinoid. Long handles continued throughout the First World War.

UMBRELLAS

By the 1870s the metal-framed umbrella was well established. A tightly rolled umbrella was practical and ornamental, and better suited to a gentleman's top hat and frock coat than the slightly raffish cane. In 1895 the *Tailor and Cutter* noted: 'Closely rolled umbrellas will be seen more frequently than ever before. Fashionable men are already wedded to them.' Most of the improvements in umbrellas during the next forty years or so were aimed at making the umbrella slimmer and more compact. Nearly all were based on the Paragon frame.

In 1894 the *Tailor and Cutter* enthused about the 'Floyce' umbrella, made by the Patent Small Rolling Umbrella Company of Moorgate, London, and claimed it to be the 'smallest rolling-up umbrella in existence', ranging from half an inch to three quarters of an inch in diameter between ferrule and band. Others mentioned were the 'Patent Supreme', with six ribs and a triangular stick, the 'Titania' with a gutta-percha-covered steel tubular stick, the automatically opening 'Ne Plus Ultra' and the automatically closing 'Automatic' umbrella, which was especially useful 'when it is impossible to use both hands, as frequently happens with business gentlemen who have sample cases to carry wherever they go'. Some sticks were fluted to take both ribs and stretchers.

From the 1890s onwards catalogues produced by department stores give some indication of the most saleable lines in umbrellas. Sears, Roebuck & Co., of Chicago, advertised as the 'Cheapest Supply House on Earth', showed mainly hook-handled umbrellas for men in 1902, and for women hooks and cross shapes with loose knots of congo and 'Princess' handles, trumpet-shaped, in mother-of-pearl or wood. Nearly all have steel sticks with Paragon-type frames. One page in the 1907 catalogue of the Army and Navy Stores, London, illustrates 47 varieties of umbrella handle, including: seventeen hooks, fifteen crutches, two button-tops and one ring-handle. Gamage's 1913 catalogue similarly

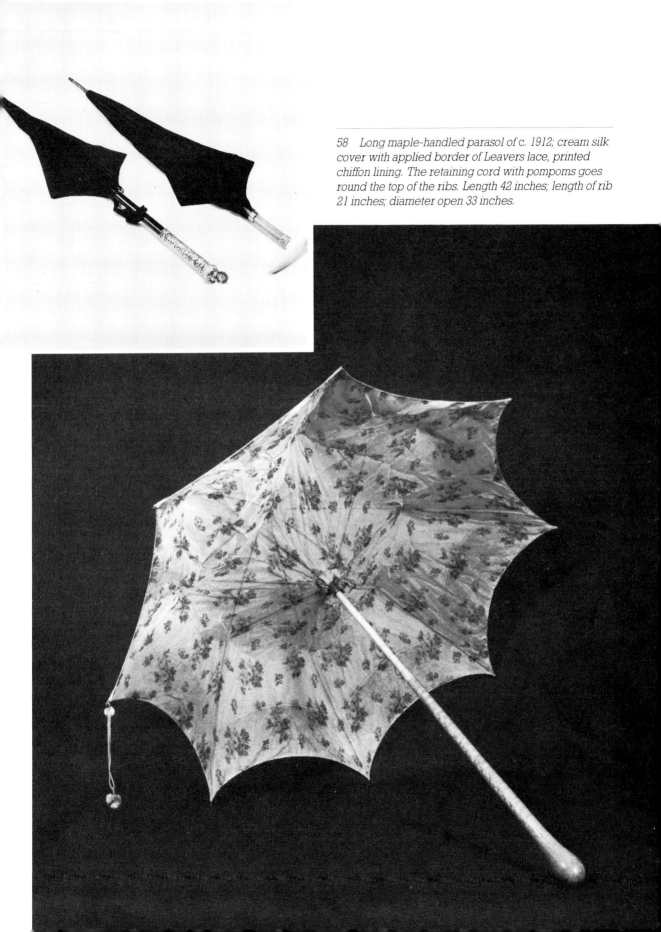

58 Long maple-handled parasol of c. 1912; cream silk cover with applied border of Leavers lace, printed chiffon lining. The retaining cord with pompoms goes round the top of the ribs. Length 42 inches; length of rib 21 inches; diameter open 33 inches.

shows mostly hooks, some carved with birds' heads, for women; and for men the L-shape popular after 1900 and a 'new' straight handle, which is probably the forerunner of 'La Militaire' of the First World War: a straight-handled umbrella with a leather loop, carried under the arm by both sexes like a civilian equivalent of the military swagger-stick. It survived into the 1920s as a sports or country umbrella.

The preponderance of hooks did not go unnoticed: 'nine out of every ten women in the tubes and trams around London favour the hook or crutch. The straight handle with knob or cap is more used by the well-to-do woman who usually has her hands free for carrying an umbrella.'[40] By 1910 only elderly men still carried heavy silver-knobbed umbrellas, and crutch, crook and cross handles were disappearing. In 1907 a new shape, the 'King Edward', a variation on the pistol butt, made a brief appearance.[41] Men's umbrella handles were of horn, antler, tortoiseshell, malacca or ivory (particularly in the 1880s and in 1910), usually on a stem of wood or cane. In 1894 the *Tailor and Cutter* illustrated mostly knob handles in bamboo, cherry, myrtle, gorse, ash and orange. Depending on their quality, all handles might have caps and bands of plain or chased gold, copper-gilt or silver: 'Silver being now so cheap, a very handsomely silver mounted handle can be given at a price that a year ago would have been thought impossible.'[42] Leather-covered handles became increasingly fashionable. In 1907 the firm of T.R. Croger used Russian leather, pigskin, crocodile and lizard; plaited leather ball

handles, to match the costume, were available for women.[43] Sticks for all handles were of lancewood or steel.

There was more variety in the handles of women's umbrellas. In 1883 onyx, cornelian, silver and painted porcelain balls were fashionable, together with 'a large ring handle in silver which is very popular and worn on the wrist'.[44] Birds' heads were fashionable in 1887, and crocodolite balls in claw settings. The Parisian 'Boulanger' umbrella, named after the French general, had a sabre-hilt-shaped handle. Carved ivory figures, pierrots, geishas or Hindu goddesses, were also seen, but these and the 'very fantastic handles with rats, mice and monkeys climbing about them'[45] of 1884 were more likely to be for the *en-tout-cas*. Watches were set into

---

59 *Women's umbrella handles.* Left to right: *tortoiseshell, gilt band, cane stem, leather strap, 'La Militaire' type, 1915 – 25, Laurus frame, labelled 'J. Pinder, Brighouse'. Composition Y-shape with agate ball ends, cane stem, brass bands, 1890–1910. Silver ball knob, 1893, cane stem, labelled 'Kendall' (the famous umbrella making firm of Leicester). Ebonized whangee, copper-gilt band inscribed '1848–1898', lock-rib frame. Bone with copper-gilt bar, cane stick, 1890–1910, labelled 'Kendall'. Silver bird's head, 1906, partridge cane stem, Laurus frame, labelled 'Bradwell Bros, Sheffield'. Handle lengths 8/8¼/8¼/8½/7¼/8½ inches; umbrella lengths 35¾/35¾/35/35½/34/35¼ inches; rib lengths 22-23 inches.*

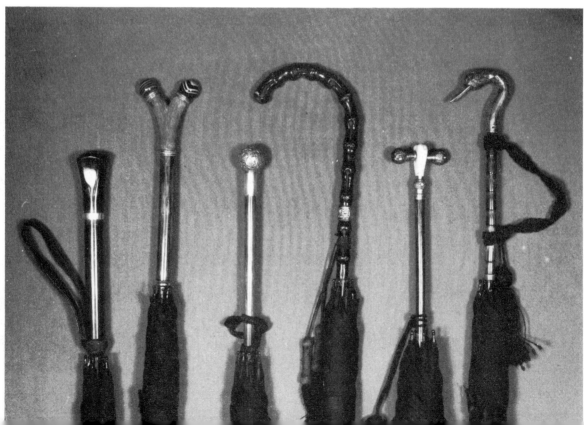

71

handles in 1887 'so that one can time a call exactly, and have no excuse for unpunctuality'.[46] Grander handles appear midway through the 1890s. In 1895, umbrellas with 'crutch handles or knobs of gun metal, starred or initialled in rose diamonds' had emerald-eyed gold serpents to hold them closed.[47] Silver animal and birds' heads, seals, owls, cockerels, with glass eyes, were popular in 1898, together with carved heads 'so arranged that by pressing on a spring the duck, dog or donkey will open its mouth'.[48] These heads were probably made up to the First World War, though mechanical heads were described as the 'very latest thing' in March 1909.[49] On a brown-and-black umbrella in Bath is a plastic poodle head which, when a lever is pressed at the back, sticks out its tongue. The silver band bears the date letter for 1903. Many umbrellas and en-tout-cas with fine quality or mechanical heads are also inscribed 'Brigg & Sons, London', the name of a famous firm of umbrella makers which, as Swaine, Adeney, Brigg & Co. since 1943, still occupies premises in Piccadilly, London.

The great tide of invention that brought electric light, the telephone, the motor car and the aeroplane, all within thirty years around 1900, created a few ripples in the world of umbrellas. Ingenious handles were designed, often patented, and made, probably in very small quantities, for an interested public. Some of the ideas were bizarre: a handle in 1900, for instance, shaped as a human head with open mouth to take a cigar or cigarette and a pump to keep it alight, or the memorial handles in 1911, carved with portraits of dead husbands for American widows. Others were more practical: the pepper sprinkler for stopping dog fights, or the 'Pathfinder' which incorporated a torch. Some umbrella handles unscrewed; some had receptacles for matches, pins and needles. One, in 1908, had the owner's portrait on the porcelain lid to a recess containing a powder puff.

Walking-stick umbrellas in telescopic cases, an adaptation of an idea of 1809, were patented in 1872, and were still being made in the 1960s. Other designs had non-collapsing cases of wood or leather. C.H. Dumenil and W.H. Brigg (of Brigg & Sons) patented in 1894 a

---

60 Page of men's umbrellas from a Gamage's catalogue of 1913; by this time the hook handle was called a 'crook'.

61 Page of women's umbrellas from a Gamage's catalogue of 1913.

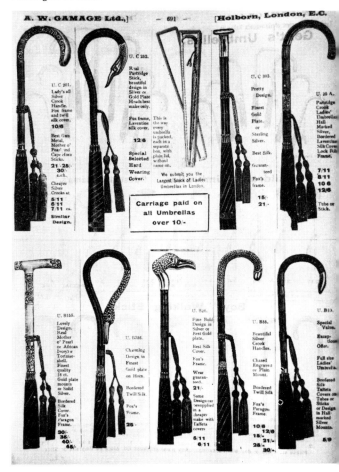

walking stick fitted with a pencil under a hinged oval flap.[50] Adapted for the umbrella, it is made and sold today as a 'racing umbrella'. Swaine and Adeney advertised these umbrellas with pigskin-covered handles for 48s. each gentleman's size, 45s. lady's size, in the *Field* in 1912. A silk umbrella with a rattan cane handle and silver mount cost 30s. or 27s. respectively. An umbrella fitted with a horse-measuring stick (patented in 1903) was also sold. Other accessories for the sporting life included the combination umbrella and shooting stick, probably invented in the 1890s. The hook or loop handle in two parts opened flat to form a seat; the ferrule is spiked to stick into the ground. The Army and Navy Stores' 1907 catalogue illustrates the 'Cunliffe' model which weighed about 1½lb and cost 33s. 6d. for ladies, £2 and 36s. 6d. for gentlemen. Leather-covered handles were 3s. extra.

Covers were mostly domed, although in 1908 it is reported: 'Hitherto public taste in all countries has favoured the umbrella with many ribs, whereas at the present the fashion seems to be inclining to those with few ribs',[51] the choice being between the high dome and the flat shape. This is perhaps more applicable to the *en-tout-cas* than the umbrella, as all the umbrellas examined of the period had the standard eight ribs. American covers, however, were often eccentric. In 1910 the 'Aeroplane' umbrella had a French-carved ivory handle portraying aviators such as Bleriot or Wright, and two of its six ribs shorter to make an aeroplane-wing shape.[52] Other shapes had anything from four to 12 or 16 ribs.

Materials were various: gloria from 1870, laventine, Spitalfields from 1878, and so forth, most of them now unidentifiable. In his diary in April 1876 the Reverend Francis Kilvert recorded: 'No sooner had Lady Hereford and her party gone than I found she had taken my umbrella and left me with a much better one, a fine silk umbrella in place of my zenilla.'[53] 'Zenilla' is probably a misreading for zanella, a silk and wool mixture first produced in 1848 and popular in the 1870s and 1880s. Covers were invariably black or brown, but in 1908 colours, particularly green, were again fashionable for women.

THE *EN-TOUT-CAS*

As in the previous period, the *en-tout-cas* is elusive. In general it has an elaborate or costly handle and a plain cover. The borderline between the *en-tout-cas* and the plain parasol is very narrow and depends on the waterproofing of the silk.

In 1879 an *en-tout-cas* of black silk with an ebony and nickel handle was also called a 'portmanteau sunshade' because it could be packed in a moderate size trunk.[54] In

62 Left: *man's umbrella; partridge cane, silver band, 1913. The rib tips are the pattern introduced in 1910, labelled 'J. Wade . . . Leeds'.* Right: *The 'Tank Umbrella', c. 1916, L-shaped furze handle, labelled 'Bradwell Bros, Sheffield'. The original wrapper has a picture of a First World War tank and Regd. No. 392068; the price was 6s. 6d. reduced to 5s. 11d.*

1880 a primrose-bordered brown *en-tout-cas* was carried with a seal-brown cashmere costume embroidered with polka dots. Ecru, red and wine-coloured *en-tout-cas* were fashionable in 1885, as well as shot colours such as red and black. Black-and-white moiré-covered *en-tout-cas* were popular in 1888 and in 1889, with 'a very superior description of handles or tops in ivory, coral or carved wood'.[55] *En-tout-cas* of this date are 39 or 40 inches in length, large and often covered with striped silk in two colours. In 1896 grosgrain, dark blue, brown, dark green, or even scarlet, is recommended for wear with tailor-made costumes, with shot *merveilleux* or *chiné* to go with lighter toilettes. Many of the light, plain sunshades seen in photographs of summer functions in this period might well be *en-tout-cas* (see fig. 49). *En-tout-cas* and sunshades are often listed together in store catalogues. In the Junior Army and Navy Stores 1894 catalogue the only *en-tout-cas* specifically mentioned is in shot silk with a plain or carved handle costing from 6s. 6d. to 21s. 6d. In the Army and Navy Store's 1907 catalogue all the *en-tout-cas* listed are black, in twill, grosgrain and moiré, but re-coverings could be had in any colour. Rib lengths were 20½- and 21½-inch for an *en-tout-cas*, 23-inch for a lady's, and 25- to 27½-inch for a gentleman's umbrella. Some *en-tout-cas* could be very elaborate: one in the *Ladies Field* in 1907 is shot grey-and-biscuit silk 'lined with chiffon in pink and blue pastel tones, with a border of Cluny lace and raised appliqués of white crochet'. Sunshades with chiffon linings appeared in the 1907 Army and Navy Stores' catalogue.

As umbrellas became more colourful after 1908, the *en-tout-cas* tended to lose whatever separate identity it had.

CARRIAGE PARASOLS AND MOTOR SUNSHADES

In 1906 the *Queen* noticed the return of the small carriage parasol. It was described in 1907 as 'the exact counterpart of those actually used in the early Victorian days',[56] with an ivory folding stick and a cover of painted chiffon over silk edged with chiffon frills. Two similar parasols, described as French, are in the Victoria & Albert Museum. Were it not for their typically Edwardian covers of machine-embroidered net or silk muslin, they could be mistaken for parasols of the 1870s; indeed, older frames could have been re-covered to suit the fashion.

Horse-drawn carriages were being superseded by the automobile in the early 1900s. Edward VII, as Prince of Wales, had bought a motorized dog-cart soon after the first international show of 'horseless carriages' at the Crystal Palace in 1896, and in 1901 ordered from Daimler a car to hold six persons, a driver and a footman. By 1906 cars were large and reasonably comfortable, and many establishments had a chauffeur on the staff, even if the master or mistress drove themselves.

Parasol manufacturers responded to the new vehicle and the need to protect the face from wind and dust in the same way as they had done in 1838. The carriage parasol of 1908 with a crook handle, folding stick, tilting or marquise head and a frilled silk cover[57] was very similar to the 'New Motor Sunshade' in Gamage's 1913 catalogue. That could be supplied in all colours for 10s. 6d., or, lined to match the car, for 12s. 6d. It is similar to the parasols of the 1880s except that it folds. Handles on motor sunshades are always larger than those of carriage parasols. In the same catalogue, the new 'Auto' motor car shade has a green, navy or black cover, a marquise hinge, and when not in use folds up and packs inside a leather case 'to hang on the arm or in the car'. The principle is very similar to that of the 'Piccolo' umbrella, registered as a design by J.C. Vickery in 1909.[58] In its commonest form it is a gilt-metal-mounted wooden tubular case with a pull-off cap, containing a metal marquise frame with coloured silk cover on a metal stick which screws into the closed end of the case forming the handle. An oval rosette of silk and a cord loop are attached to the case (see fig. 64). Variations in the way of carved heads instead of the cap are quite common; both the Victoria & Albert Museum and the

63 Motor sunshade, 1910–20; cream plastic and ebonized wood handle, marquise hinge at the top, silk cover, solid metal rib frame labelled 'S. Fox & Co. Ltd Arcus'.

City of Birmingham Museum have ones with dog's-head caps, and after 1910 some cases were ribbon-covered. Larger motor shades are also seen, recognizable by the presence of the marquise hinge. One in Cheltenham Museum has a rosewood handle with purple-and-white plastic top and bands, a black-japanned solid frame and a green silk cover. The handle is jointed under a screw-fitting to fold flat.

Motor shades disappeared with faster and more enclosed cars, though they were made into the 1920s. A Brigg & Sons motor shade with a purple ball handle and a white-and-purple checked cover in the Gallery of English Costume, Manchester, has a silver band hallmarked for 1922.

CHILDREN'S SUNSHADES AND UMBRELLAS

Until the advent of the larger parasol it is difficult to identify children's sunshades, as in size they would not be much smaller than the fashionable parasol. From the 1880s, however, sunshades which are recognizably for children appeared. They usually have solid frames,

64   'Piccolo' umbrella, c. 1909; marked 'J.C. Vickery, Regent St, W, Rd No. 549864' (registered about 24 September 1909); maple wood case, gilt bands, blue silk cover on seven ribs. The umbrella part unscrews from the closed end of the case and, when not in use, is kept in it.

65   Japanese sunshade, from the Girl's Own Paper, 1884.

The child's umbrella is often a miniature version of an adult's, similarly covered with silk, cotton and wool mixtures, nylon from the 1950s, and printed plastic, for girls' umbrellas, from the 1960s onwards.

JAPANESE SUNSHADES

After centuries of virtual isolation, Japan and her products came to public attention at the International Exhibition of 1862. But it is probably from 1868, when a commercial treaty was signed between Great Britain and Japan, that Japanese sunshades entered this country. Of the oriental warehouses which flourished to meet the demand, Arthur Liberty's, established as East India House, Regent Street, London in 1875, was the most famous and the most enduring. Japanese sunshades were often featured in paintings and magazine illustrations in the late 1870s, and in 1879 the *Milliner and Dressmaker* noted 'the soft flowered or plain silks and the fans and parasols from Japan being used a great deal'.

The Japanese sunshade (see fig. 65) has a bamboo stick and a large number of ribs cut from one piece of bamboo. The cover of thin paper, which may be made from cotton rags, rice or maize straw, or, in the best, from the bark bast of the mulberry tree,[59] is painted in colours mixed with alum and trapped between two layers of the ribs. The stretchers are thin strips of wood or bamboo held together by a multiplicity of cotton threads. Occasional examples are found in which the cover has been waterproofed with oil or varnish. They were cheap; a Liberty's employee could remember selling two cases of them at 1s. each on a Bank Holiday at the Alexandra Palace,[60] and in about 1910 the Eastern and Indian Embroideries Association advertised coloured sunshades 33 inches across at 5s. 9d. per dozen. Some were very large, nine feet across, for covering a bazaar stall or for garden use.

Japanese sunshades have always been popular, particularly at the seaside, but it is only occasionally that they have become fashionable – in the late 1870s and 1880s, the 1920s and the late 1970s. Most of the large number of these sunshades in museum collections date from the 1920s (as most are marked 'Made in Japan' or 'Nippon', they must have been made after 1891); few, if any, from the period before.

plain wood or cane handles and printed cotton covers. They were cheaply made and sold, as they were not expected to last. One in the Birmingham City Museum has a fawn cotton cover printed with pairs of flower fairies; another in a private collection on display at Hanbury Hall, Worcestershire, is printed with Kate Greenaway children feeding geese. Children's parasols are listed in the Sears, Roebuck & Co. 1902 catalogue with 10- to 18-inch ribs and priced from 18 to 99 cents; some are covered in silk.

Children's umbrellas can usually only be traced from store or trade catalogues. According to one, they were made on Fox's 18½-inch Paragon ribs for children up to nine years old, and on 20-inch ribs for nine to fourteen years old, but the Army and Navy Stores' 1907 catalogue listed plain umbrellas for children on 20- and 22-inch ribs, with more ornamental handles for girls on 18- to 22-inch ribs. Youths' umbrellas on 23- and 25-inch ribs are the same size as ladies', or the smallest size of gentlemen's umbrellas. Many of the plain handles are hooks and could be mounted in gilt metal or silver. Animal heads were a feature of children's umbrellas, 'Just like Mama's', in the 1913 Gamage's catalogue, and cost from 2s.11d. to 10s. 6d. They continued to be popular.

6

1920-1984

PARASOLS

Just before the First World War, in 1912 and 1913, there was a brief flirtation with the oriental flat-shaped parasol and with bright colours, perhaps under the influence of Diaghilev's Russian Ballet and Leon Bakst's barbaric designs for *Scheherazade*, produced in Paris in 1910. Periodicals such as the *Journal des Dames et des Modes* published plates of parasols covered in hand-painted silks or printed cretonnes in bright colours with flowers against geometric or grid backgrounds. Although the Great War does not seem to have affected production in the same way that the Second World War was to do, it nevertheless had a sobering effect on fashions, and such parasols as were made had either plain or simply bordered covers.

In June 1919 the *Bag, Portmanteau and Umbrella Trader* reported: 'For the first time since 1914 there are occasions for carrying "dressy" parasols.' The flat, Japanese style was revived with covers of cretonne or shantung silk printed with Chinese or Japanese scenes and Futurist designs in bright colours. Dome shapes were flatter, and ribs numbered between eight and 24. Rib tips had been made to match handles since 1910, but after about 1914 they became a feature in their own right. In 1919 it was reported that, 'in nearly every case of these high-class goods the rib ends are of some "ivory" material and are of heavy square or hexagonal form nearly an inch long'.[1] They were a feature of parasols, umbrellas and *en-tout-cas* until at least the mid-1920s. By 1927 they were considerably shorter. Most were made of various plastics but some were of richer materials: 2½- inch-long tips in eight varieties of agate on one parasol, for instance. The number and size of the tips necessitated a thicker stick and handle. Carved wood

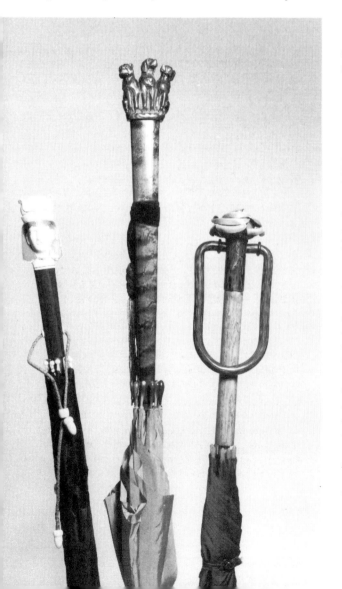

66　Handles on en-tout-cas, *1910–20*. Left: *ivory carved as an Egyptian pharoah's head above wood, lancewood stick, Paragon frame with ivory rib tips, navy-blue silk cover with ribbed edge. Egyptian motifs were popular even before the discovery of Tutankhamen's tomb in 1923*. Centre: *horn carved as three seated dogs, oval section maple stem, gilt Paragon-type frame with horn rib tips, shot fawn silk cover*. Right: *plastic rose, plastic loop handle as rose stem, wood stick, Paragon-type frame with horn or plastic rib tips, brown silk cover with deep-ribbed band. All from a collection of fourteen parasols, umbrellas and* en-tout-cas *which belonged to Cara Leland Broughton, Lady Fairhaven (died 1939), daughter of an American millionaire.*

and ivory, and moulded plastics and composition were called into use, and their decoration reflected the enthusiasms of the day: Japanese and Chinese figures or motifs, Egyptian deities, especially after the discovery of Tutankhamen's tomb in 1923, flowers and geometric shapes in the Art Deco style after the Exposition des Arts Decoratifs in Paris in 1925. Long thin sticks with tapering 'billiard-cue' or onion-shaped handles continued into the mid-1920s. From 1921, although the handle stayed long, the frame diminished in size.

The innovation of the post-war years was the short parasol, which, with the short umbrella, probably developed from 'La Militaire', a straight-handled umbrella intended to be carried under the arm. By May 1919 short stubby parasols with straight wooden handles decorated with coloured pokerwork were on sale at the boutique Au Printemps in Paris. In 1924 the *Tatler* reported: 'As the hats increase in size the sunshades

67   Crêpe de Chine cover printed with pink roses and grey-green grapes, c. 1921. Bright colours and large patterns were fashionable in the early 1920s. The weight of this fabric is such that the parasol could have been made of dress material to match a dress; the cane handle is long.

become ridiculously smaller. A novelty this season are those of silk trimmed with beads.' Handles were of plaited braid, shagreen relieved with ivory, and ebony. Throughout the remainder of the 1920s and early 1930s it was these shorter parasols rather than the long-handled ones that were the most fashionable. They were lavishly and often humorously decorated. One, which appears in a fashion drawing of 1927, for instance, has the head of a Chinaman as the handle and his feet as the ferrule; another, a year later, was carved as a palm tree. Handles were very thick and like the long handles reflect the crazes of the day. Covers were inverted saucer-shape or flat, with eight to 16 ribs, sometimes with droplet-shaped tips. The thinner fabrics of the period: georgette, crêpe de Chine, lawn, and net, are all used; printed, ruched or shaded so that colours range from the palest at the edge to the darkest at the centre. Some are frilled, some resemble flowers; a parasol with 12 ribs, one of a collection in the Victoria & Albert Museum from a Belgian manufacturer, has a centre of ruched white georgette amid silk petals creased along the centres so that they stand up. Parasols of woven raffia with flowers embroidered in coloured raffia were also popular. Rich fabrics were not used, reflecting the parasol's new role as a plaything rather than a status symbol.

The freedom and independence that many women had experienced by doing war-work in factories and the like did not find full expression in dress until 1925 when skirts, which had hovered about the ankles since the war, shot upwards. Arms and necks had been uncovered in daytime some while before, and as the health-giving properties of sunlight were realized the parasol's active role began to diminish. Smart Americans were making the winter resorts of the the French Riviera fashionable in summertime and by the later 1920s a suntan had become as much a status symbol as the carriage parasol had been before, as it implied sufficient

wealth to holiday abroad. By the early 1930s the fashionable parasol was carried only with formal day dresses at garden parties and race meetings such as Ascot. From 1924, in the rather throwaway style affected by fashion writers, it was a mere 'sunshade', and is rarely described in detail. In 1927 the American Sears and Roebuck catalogue listed no parasols, only 'parasol-umbrellas'.

There have been one or two attempts at revival, usually associated with a romantic style of costume. In July 1938 King George VI and Queen Elizabeth paid a state visit to France. At a performance of ballet by the lakeside, 'the Queen opened a parasol of transparent lace and tulle and delighted all the onlookers. At a stroke, she resuscitated the art of the parasol makers of Paris and London.'[2] The revival was short-lived. Lace and chiffon parasols are recorded during the summer of 1939, but on 3 September France and Great Britain declared war on Germany, and the Second World War had begun.

War, clothes rationing and the square-shouldered military style that women had worn for so long created a nostalgia for full-skirted feminine clothes, memorably realized in Christian Dior's La Ligne Corolle, the New Look of 1947. In 1946 Cecil Beaton photographed the model Carmen for *Vogue* wearing a wide-brimmed hat, mittens and a dress of *broderie anglaise*. The matching, frilled parasol she carried had what appears to be a glass or Perspex hook handle. During the 1950s parasols appear spasmodically, associated with crisp, full-skirted summer dresses worn over stiffened petticoats and a revived crinoline. In 1954 a long-handled parasol with a frilled, spotted cover, by Liberty, was teamed with a coat-dress and a small white-and-biscuit-coloured straw hat. In 1956 a light-coloured parasol covered with black lace was carried with a summer dress of hyacinth-blue pleated nylon, both retailed by Susan Small. Fewer parasols appear in the 1960s. In 1965 Charles Judson supplied lace-edged white parasols for a *fête champêtre* photographed for the July issue of *Vogue*. By 1967 what looks like a parasol carried with clothes and expressing 'the upsurge of romantic feeling in the world of fashion'[3] was described as a white umbrella, and in June 1974 the chiffon and lace parasol, appearing with a Bellville-Sassoon white crêpe de Chine and lace 'Edwardian' dress, was hired.[4] Parasols can probably still be bought, made to order, but their place as an accessory has been taken by the umbrella and the bottle of sun-tan lotion.

UMBRELLAS
The fashionable style during the First World War was La Militaire, an umbrella with a straight handle and leather

68 Pokerwork wood handle painted in green and orange, c. 1930. Sixteen-rib frame which opens flat, green plastic rib tips, green crêpe de Chine cover.

69 Umbrellas. Left: *probably a child's; partridge cane,* ▷
silver band, black taffeta cover, 1911. Length 30½
inches; rib length 19 inches; diameter open 32 inches.
Centre: woman's; wood hook handle, sterling silver tip
cup, 1936–40. Black silk or rayon cover with black satin
band and narrow white edge, frame marked 'Patent
No. 420709 S. Fox & Co. Ltd'. Length 30 inches; rib
length 20 inches; diameter open 33½ inches. Right:
woman's; leather-covered pistol butt handle with strap,
1930–40. Brown silk cover over ten ribs, leather case.
Marked 'Made in Vienna'. Length 23½ inches; rib
length 19½ inches; diameter open 33½ inches.

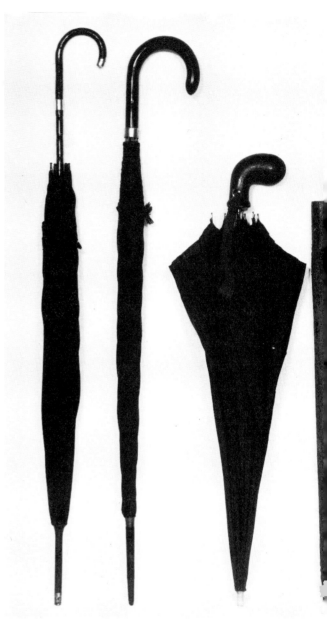

loop. It was carried under the arm. In June 1918 the *Bag,
Portmanteau and Umbrella Trader* reported, 'Perhaps
some people are getting just a little tired of La Militaire
style, it is so universally used now both for men and
women, but however popular the hook may become
again it can never oust the other from its assured
popularity, which is founded on extreme utility.'
Although this is largely true for women's umbrellas, it is
not true for men's. In May 1919, though men's umbrellas
apparently had knob handles carved as animal heads or
helmeted firemen, by July when there was a run on
umbrellas, probably due to 'the return of the top hat to
popular favour',[5] the hook was the favourite handle, as it
has been ever since.

In the years between the two World Wars an umbrella
was part of the unofficial uniform of a gentleman in
London. 'Not to have worn a hat, a bowler, a trilby or a
topper in the West End and especially "in the Season"
was considered in the Brigade of Guards to be
improperly dressed. In addition to the hat officers also
had to carry a tightly rolled umbrella. Any kind of parcel
was taboo, even a small one.'[6] Not only officers, but
civilians too, and anyone who aspired to be smartly
dressed. Nearly all the men appearing in photographs in
the *Tailor and Cutter* between 1932 and 1943 carry
umbrellas. Such umbrellas were of black silk or silk and
cotton mixture, with whangee, malacca or pigskin-
covered handles, sometimes with gold-plated or silver
mounts. Many of the better-quality ones were on wood or
cane sticks, cheaper 'small-rolling umbrellas' being on
steel tubes. In 1936 the difference in price in a John
Barker and Co. catalogue was between 45s. for a cane
stick and *glacé* silk cover, and 16s. 6d. for a metal stick
and a mixture cover. Just before the Second World War
the Army and Navy Stores offered a wide range of men's
umbrellas, from natural woods, leather-covered,
partridge cane, pimento, malacca, snakewood, cape
horn and shagreen; to ivory- and tortoiseshell-veneered
handles ranging in price from 100 and 105s. for the latter,

down to 19s. Every one is a hook. After the war there was
less choice; Barker's, who had offered whangee,
malacca and natural wood before, offered only natural
and stained wood handles and cotton taffeta covers in
1951. This was due in part to the difficulty in getting
materials after the war, but also in part to crippling
purchase tax.

The same attitudes prevailed after the Second World
War as after the First. In *Family Album*, published in
1960, the Duke of Windsor wrote: 'The rolled-up
umbrella is still *de rigueur* for Guards officers and city

men,' and this was copied all down the social scale. There is in fact very little difference between men's umbrellas before and after the war until the arrival of nylon. Both Harrods and Austin Reed advertised nylon-covered umbrellas for men in 1955. Waterproof, strong and less subject to rot than silk or cotton, nylon gradually came to replace both, although all three were available on umbrellas up to the mid-1970s.

Subsequent developments have been aimed at making the umbrella more efficient or more compact. In the early 1960s Hornes advertised the 'Press Button Umbrella' with a nylon cover, malacca or whangee handle, and an Italian frame, at 85s.[7] Other models followed, with real leather-covered handles, or plastic copies. 'Growy' umbrellas with folding ribs and telescopic sticks also appeared for men in the 1960s, but both they and the later 'Knirps' were only slowly adopted as practicality conquered umbrella mystique. Most of the telescopic and automatic-opening umbrellas for sale in Britain are made abroad, in Taiwan, Hong Kong or Korea. But men's umbrellas, with wood sticks and hook handles in a wide variety of natural and sand-scorched woods, and some leather-covered handles, are still made by hand in this country by firms such as T. Fox & Co. Ltd, and James Smith & Co. Ltd. Recently, as regards men's traditional umbrellas, there has been a return to what is almost a pistol-butt handle in hazel and ash, using the natural wood with the bark left on.

At the end of the First World War women's umbrellas were long, either of La Militaire type or with a hook handle. Both silver ball knobs with regimental badges and ivory hook handles were advertised, by Swaine and Adeney, on malacca with silk covers and Fox's frames, in 1918.[8] The hook-handled umbrella had a thick spike of wood, but the band, rib tips, open cap and ferrule were all of ivory. Ivory was particularly fashionable in Paris in 1919, carved in Japanese style with monkeys, or engraved with Egyptian desert scenes. Imitation ivory was used on cheaper models. La Militaire began to lose its military look at this time; it became shorter and lost its ferrule. The leather strap, which had been either a wrist loop or long enough to be passed over one shoulder and under the arm, was replaced by a cord holder which lay flat against the stick or passed through a hole in the handle itself. By 1921 all La Militaire styles were small; by 1923 they were common enough to be satirized by *Punch* and by 1924 they had acquired the nickname 'chubby'.

These short umbrellas were the coming fashion, but both the short and the long styles have been offered as alternatives for women's umbrellas ever since, with first one and then the other at the forefront. In the 1920s and for most of the 1930s the short umbrella occupied that

position and the long umbrella became more utilitarian. In 1925, with a hook handle, tightly rolled cover and spike, it was described as 'mannish looking . . . to accompany the mannish mode'.[9] In 1936 John Barker & Co. were offering a hook-handled umbrella in walking length or chubby style in malacca, whangee or natural ash, but the small-rolling 'pencil-slim' umbrella, in the same catalogue, heralded the return of the long umbrella to fashion.

In was ironic that as soon as women had achieved a measure of emancipation in dress, with shorter skirts and a slimmer silhouette, they should be hampered by accessories. In addition to buttonless coats that had to be held closed, and gloves, they had to carry both the clutch bag and the short umbrella under the arm. The *soignée* look of so many women in the late 1920s and 1930s must have taken a lot of practice! Like the short parasol, but to an even greater extent, since covers were plain, the attraction and the value of the short umbrella lay in its handle. They were all short and thick, sometimes a cylinder banded in different colours, round or oval in section. Much composition (sometimes abbreviated to 'compo') was used, moulded and brightly coloured. Horn, ivory, wood inset with plastic, and leather-covered handles were all to be found. In general the handles of the 1920s are curvaceous and florid and those of the 1930s are angular or geometric, but this is not an invariable rule, for Asprey & Co. advertised in 1924 tapering or hexagonal-section handles with a short ferrule to match. Novelty heads reappeared after the war in carved wood or plastic and are mentioned fairly frequently in fashion reports. In 1925, for instance, a dog's head with a leather-belted monkey-fur collar was noted;[10] Airedale and fox- and wire-haired terrier heads were available from the Army and Navy Stores in 1937. Some of these heads had moveable jaws, and sometimes the whole dog, not just the head, was represented. Bird-head handles appeared too, in the 1920s, sometimes with a bangle in the beak forming a rigid sort of wrist loop. All short umbrellas have a strap of some sort; either leather attached to a small metal ring on the handle, or cord pushed as a single or double thickness through a hole in

the handle and knotted, with acorn-shaped finials. Towards the end of the 1930s 'dog collar' handles, a leather strap slotted through the handle and buckled, and leather-covered handles with a loop attached to the top, both came into fashion.[11] Some of these short umbrellas are so small that they were combined with handbags to form 'Bagbrellas'.

Most of the small umbrellas were either flat, shallow-domed or a mushroom shape (the latter called 'Luxon' in America in 1927), when open. The covers are either plain, in black, navy or dark brown, or have a small check pattern. Other colours such as green and red were also available.

The *en-tout-cas* by this time had merged with the umbrella. In an Asprey's catalogue for 1930 all short umbrellas were described as *en-tout-cas*, and in the 1927 Sears and Roebuck catalogue only short 'Parasol-Umbrellas' were listed. Elsewhere, in Barker's and the Army and Navy Stores' catalogues, for instance, they were 'chubby' umbrellas. There seems to be no difference in the covers, for most were plain silk or silk and cotton mixture, only the parasol-umbrella having a wide two-tone border. In the 1930s rayon appeared as a substitute for silk in umbrella covers, rather later than it had first been used for dresses.

Some of the Sears and Roebuck parasol-umbrellas are described as 'stub' size, to fit into a 24-inch suitcase. Size was obviously a preoccupation of the period, as a number of telescopic models are listed in catalogues and survive in museums. The 1930 Asprey's catalogue showed a 'Telescopic Portable Umbrella' with a leather or ivory handle and ferrule or a small, cylindrical shagreen and ivory handle. An umbrella in the Museum of London, which is said to be a child's, of about 1924, has a plastic pistol-butt handle, a chromium-plated telescopic stick, ribs hinged to fold downwards and stretchers with a supplementary rod up to the top notch. The cover is satin-striped pink silk with a cream edge. Another telescopic model, in Nottingham Costume Museum, was brought back from America in 1932. It has an aluminium stick, ribs that fold upwards when closed and an amber-coloured plastic handle. The cover is brown rayon. It is marked: 'Am. Fold. Umb. Corp, Pat. 1911784, Made in U.S.A.' The Growy umbrella, 'a fullsized umbrella that folds into a handbag', appeared in Barker's catalogue for 1936.

The walking-length umbrella returned to fashion towards the end of the 1930s. A small-rolling 'pencil-slim' umbrella with an ivory 'thimble' top appears in the Barker's catalogue for 1936, and the Army and Navy Stores offers a 'new walking length' of 33 inches in 1937. Some of these larger umbrellas have handles made of plastic or covered with snakeskin or pigskin to tone with

◁ 70 *Ivory button top carved with bird's head, thick malacca stem, wood stick, ten-rib Paragon frame, cased in lilac silk, ivory rib tips. Hand-stitched lilac silk cover; the silk woven by Vanners & Fennell Ltd, the* en-tout-cas *made by Cummings of Poultry and Cannons Street. A replica of one presented to Queen Mary in 1926; Queen Mary was renowned for always carrying an umbrella or* en-tout-cas *with her.*

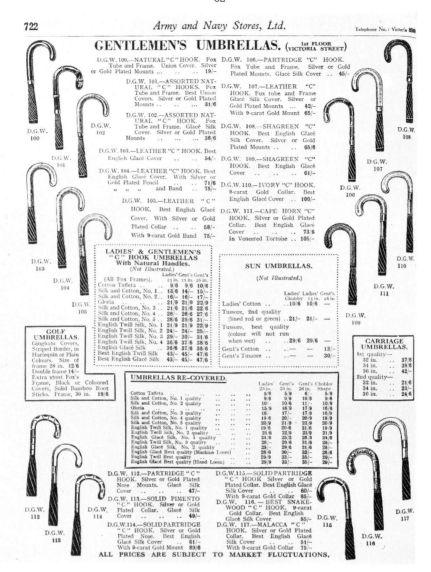

71 Men's umbrellas from the Army and Navy Stores catalogue of 1937–8.

the cover. In June 1937 the French magazine *Marie-Claire* reported: 'At Lobb's, they told me of the demise of the "Tom Thumb", the stout little umbrella which we have loved for so long.' (The Lobb's referred to was the Paris branch of the celebrated London firm of bootmakers; it sold Brigg umbrellas.)

Throughout the 1930s, the Depression and the imports of cheap umbrella parts made life very difficult for umbrella manufacturers. Many had to reduce the size and variety of their stocks. In 1935–6 S. Fox & Co. rationalized their output by producing Paragon Broad Stretcher Ribs, Patent No. 420709, which virtually superseded all their other lines (see fig. 69).[12] During the war, however, they, along with other firms, practically

ceased umbrella production, making instead goods for the war effort, and T. Fox & Co. turned to parachute manufacture. Between 1942 and 1947 umbrellas could only be made under licence. After the war, to judge from American magazines, the long umbrella was still in fashion, with either a straight or hooked handle and plain or checked covers. In the Museum of Costume & Textiles, Nottingham, is an umbrella bought in Paris in 1948 to go with Dior's New Look clothes. It has a wooden twisted square-section hook handle and a red-and-white

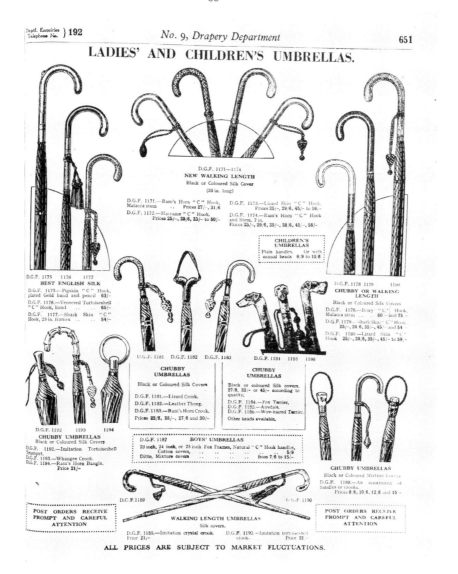

72 Ladies' and children's umbrellas from the Army and Navy Stores catalogue of 1939–40.

checked cover (see fig. 73). Stout masculine handles continued into the 1950s. A whangee-handled umbrella with a leather wrist loop and brown-checked cover was offered with a suit designed by Molyneux as first prize in a competition in *Home Chat* magazine in 1950. These handles run concurrently with slim straight handles, some with leather loops longer than the handle, or with trumpet-shaped tops. In the mid-1950s a few eccentric handles appear, carved as an African warrior's head for instance, or as ring loops or Y-shapes. A silver-finish swan's-neck-handled umbrella of 1953, made by Peter Todd Mitchell for the couture house of John Cavanagh, is in the Victoria & Albert Museum. Many of the slim-rolling umbrellas, made to be carried with slim-skirted suits,

are on metal sticks. Most umbrellas of whatever sort have cases to match the covers, so that they appear as thin as possible when rolled. Long thin hook handles in marbled plastic, or covered in leather dyed to match the cover, appear at the end of the 1950s. Many have a large tassel tied on the handle.

As with men's umbrellas, the most revolutionary change came in the cover fabric. Nylon had been invented just before the war by Du Pont in America, but most wartime production was requisitioned for

73 'New Look' umbrella, bought in Paris in 1948. Square-section hook handle, red, white and blue checked rayon cover over ten ribs. Also has matching case, bone ferrule and open cap. Length 35¼ inches; rib length 20½ inches; diameter open 36½ inches.

◁ *74 Women's umbrellas, 1960–65. Left: electro-plated metal hook handle with pattern of raised vine leaves, pale-blue nylon cover over ten ribs. Right: green leather-covered handle, green nylon cover over eight ribs, one marked 'Longlive', the trade name of the umbrella manufacturers E. Olive & Co. Ltd; woven into the selvedge on both umbrella covers is the word 'Nailon', the name for Nylon 66 as produced by Rhodialoce S.p.A., Italy, in the early to mid-1960s.*

parachutes and other essential equipment. America had nylon-covered umbrellas shortly after the war. *Harper's Bazaar* in 1949 illustrates a small, straight-bamboo-handled umbrella with a brown nylon cover in an ostrich-skin case at $22.50, and a white nylon evening umbrella at $6.

Britain probably had nylon-covered umbrellas in the early 1950s; Susan Handbags of New Bond Street, London sold them at £4 15s. each in 1954. Some of this nylon was home produced by ICI, but much was imported. Covers of the early to mid-1960s which have 'Nailon' woven into the selvedge were made of nylon 66, woven by the firm of Rhodialoce S.p.A. of Italy (see fig. 74).[13] Nylon was versatile. It could be printed or woven in a great many designs. Nowadays, through plain colours are always stocked by such manufacturers as T. Fox & Co., new patterns are chosen each year in France and

Italy to be made up for the season. Most of these designs are geometric or linear, with or without a border, but colours may change considerably from season to season. One of the most recent developments is in the use of spun nylon to give the appearance of cotton whilst retaining the hard-wearing qualities of nylon.

---

75   A selection of modern umbrellas. Left to right: metal hook, black nylon cover with printed nylon lining attached only at the ribs, 1960s onward. Pagoda, plastic and bamboo handle, printed nylon cover in blue, 1960s. Short plastic handle, checked rayon cover, 1935–40. Wood hook, plastic rib tips, printed spun nylon cover, bought at John Lewis Ltd in 1980. Wood hook, plastic rib tips, striped nylon cover. Straight wood handle with cord from ferrule to handle, nylon cover, 1983.

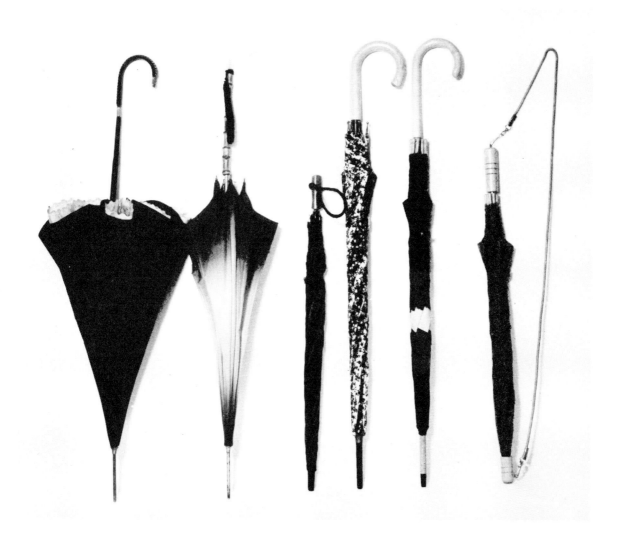

Other man-made cover fabrics have also been used. In 1938 Barker's advertised a foreign-made 'Clear-Brella', of Pliofilm, derived from rubber. It was sold in shades of red, green, blue and white at 12s. 11d., and was described as 'a great advantage in traffic'. In 1947 H.B. Dunn was granted a patent for umbrella covers in PVC, but it was not until the 1960s that a deep-domed umbrella covered in transparent plastic was produced.

In the 1970s there was a reaction against the man-made fibres and materials which had once seemed the answer to modern living. Oil shortage crises, and a 'back to natural products' movement typified by the 'peasant look', meant, in the case of umbrellas, a return to wood and cotton. Stout wooden hook handles appeared by the mid-1970s, often teamed with brightly printed cotton covers and imitation wood rib tips. An element of fun entered with duck-head handles in 1975. Umbrellas which have the snob value of being instantly identifiable as coming from certain department stores or shops have also been a feature of the umbrella scene since the 1970s. The most famous of these is probably the 'Burbrolly', so carefully made in Burberry's house check that each gore accords exactly with its neighbour. One of the most recent umbrella styles, the strap from hook or straight handle to the ferrule, appeared in *Vogue* in 1977, but took off as a popular fashion only in the early 1980s. Many of these stout-handled umbrellas are also carried by men as an alternative to the traditional hook-handled, black-covered umbrella. Large umbrellas with gores of different but bright colours, or two colours alternately, have developed from the golf umbrella, a distant cousin of the old gig umbrella.

Along with much of the textile industry, British umbrella makers have had to face up to competition from cheap imports. Umbrella parts had come into the country during the 1930s, and though required to be marked with the country or origin, many found their way into the British umbrella. In 1954 and 1955, while the industry was trying to cope with purchase tax and the after-effects of war, 'Empire Made' umbrellas were imported from Hong Kong.[14] Many were made to sell at 5s. 6d., only sixpence dearer than the tax on an average British-made umbrella. Japan exported large numbers of umbrellas in the 1960s, and since then Korea and Taiwan have followed suit. Most of the cheaper umbrellas, particularly the automatic-opening and the telescopic styles, are foreign made. Although they are bright and cheerful, they are nevertheless utilitarian and cheap enough to be easily replaced if broken. Well-made umbrellas constructed by craftsmen can still be obtained and, as many are exported, they spread the traditions of British umbrella-making round the world.

Although the umbrella has become lighter in weight and more impervious to rain due to modern scientific developments, it has not otherwise changed in essentials since Jonas Hanway first popularized it. Efforts to change its basic shape or to dispense with it entirely have met with no long-term success. It would seem that as long as there is rain there will be umbrellas, and as long as there is fashion there will be many different styles and varieties to brighten the rainy day.

Notes

CHAPTER 1

1 *Report of the Juries of the Great Exhibition, 1951,* London, 1852, pp. 655–61.
2 S. Moxon, *A Fox Centenary, Umbrella Frames, 1848–1948,* S. Fox & Co. Ltd., n.d. (*.c.* 1949), p. 15.
3 Ibid. p. 16.
4 Ibid. p. 21.
5 Information from Mr. E. Hargan, of Fox Frames Ltd.
6 The information about the frames is taken from S. Moxon, op. cit.
7 F.B. Jewell, *Veteran Sewing Machines,* David & Charles, 1975, p. 30.
8 T. Girtin, *Makers of Distinction,* Harvill Press, 1959.
9 C. Booth, *Life and Labour of the People in London,* London, 1889, ch. 9.
10 *Abridgements of Specifications relating to Umbrellas, Parasols & Walking Sticks, 1760–1866,* London, 1871.
11 S. Moxon, op., cit. p. 33.
12 C. Dickens, *Sketches by Boz, Tales,* 1836–7.
13 See V. Foster, *Bags and Purses,* Batsford, 1982, p. 36.
14 A. Adburgham, *Shops and Shopping,* Allen & Unwin, 1964, p. 111.
15 BT 51/64; I am indebted to Miss A. Houston, formerly of the Patent Office at Kew, for this information.

CHAPTER 2

1 *Inventaires des Meubles de la Rayne d'Escosse, Douairiere de France*; catalogue of the jewels, dresses, furniture, books and paintings of Mary, Queen of Scots, 1556–69, contribution of the Marquess of Dalhousie to the Bannatyne Club, Edinburgh 1883.
2 Ibid. p. 156.
3 Max von Boehn, *Modes and Manners: Ornaments,* J.M. Dent, 1929, p. 128.
4 From information kindly supplied by Janet Arnold.
5 Quoted in Octave Uzanne, *The Sunshade, the Glove, and the Muff,* Nimmo & Bain, London 1883.
6 W. Sangster, *Umbrellas and their History,* Cassell, Pelter & Galpin, n.d. (*c.* 1870), p. 37.

7 *Report of the Juries of the Great Exhibition,* London 1852, p. 656.
8 Ben Jonson, *The Devil is an Ass,* IV, *i,* 1616, quoted in W. Sangster, op. cit. p. 38.
9 Michael Drayton, *The Muses Elizium, The Second Nimphall,* quoted in T.S., Crawford, *A History of the Umbrella,* David & Charles, Newton Abbot, 1970, p. 99.
10 *The Diary of John Evelyn* (1620–1706), ed. E.S. de Beer, OUP, 1959, p. 460.
11 Ibid. p. 94.
12 Max von Boehn, op. cit. p. 136.
13 O. Uzanne, op. cit. p. 39.
14 *Report of the Juries* . . . , p. 659.
15 T.S. Crawford, op. cit. p. 99.
16 John Locke, *Travels in France, 1675–9,* ed. John Lough, CUP, 1953.
17 A. Varron, *The History of the Umbrella and the Sunshade,* an article in *Ciba Review,* No. 42, 1942, p. 1519.
18 John Evelyn, op. cit. p. 439.
19 T.S. Crawford, op. cit. p. 104.
20 T.S. Crawford, loc. cit.
21 Max von Boehn, op. cit. p. 101.
22 T.S. Crawford, op. cit. p. 101.
23 Quoted in T.S. Crawford, op. cit. p. 105.
24 W. Sangster, op. cit. p. 41.
25 C.W. & P. Cunnington, *A Handbook of Eighteenth Century Costume,* Faber & Faber, 1957, p. 179.
26 T.S. Crawford, op. cit. p. 109.
27 Kent County Record Office, *The Earl of Thanet's Accounts,* quoted in C.W. & P. Cunnington, op. cit. p. 179.

CHAPTER 3

1 *The Diary of Abigail Gawthern,* 1751–1810, ed. Adrian Henstock, Thoroton Society Record Series, vol. 33, Nottingham 1980, p. 33.
2 T.S. Crawford, *A History of the Umbrella,* David & Charles, 1970, p. 123.
3 *Wrest Park Papers,* quoted in Anne Buck, *Dress in Eighteenth Century England,* Batsford, 1979, p. 101.

4   Doris Langley Moore, *Fashion through Fashion Plates*, Ward Lock, 1971, pl. 3.
5   T.S. Crawford, op. cit. p. 120.
6   Quoted in Elizabeth McClellan, *A History of American Costume*, Tudor Publishing Co., 1969 reprint of 1904 edition, p. 230.
7   *Mrs Elizabeth Montagu, Her Letters and Friendships*, ed. R. Blunt, 1923, vol. II, p. 81, quoted in Anne Buck, op. cit. p. 100.
8   Wilkie Collins, *The Dead Secret*, 1857.
9   M. Ginsberg, *An Introduction to Fashion Illustration*, Victoria & Albert Museum, Compton Press & Pitman Publishing, 1980, pl. 29.
10   Max von Boehn, *Modes and Manners: The 18th Century*, J.M. Dent, 1929, p. 181.
11   British Patent No. 3619, 1812.
12   *Ackermann's Repository of the Arts*, August 1809, also the *Ladies' Monthly Museum*, October 1809.
13   *J.A.D. Ingres – Drawings*, Arts Council Exhibition catalogue, 1979, number 26. Victoria & Albert Museum (E230–1946).
14   'A Letter from Paris' (probably from *La Belle Assemblée*), quoted in E. McClellan, op. cit. p. 383.
15   The *Ladies' Monthly Museum*, vol. XIX, January 1824, p. 165.
16   The *World of Fashion*, August 1826, p. 286.
17   The *World of Fashion*, August 1828, p. 180.
18   Ibid.
19   The *World of Fashion*, June 1829, p. 132.
20   Charles Dickens, *The Posthumous Papers of the Pickwick Club*, 1836–7, chapter 13.
21   The *Ladies' Pocket Magazine & Gem of Fashion*, September 1833.
22   Charles Dickens, *Sketches by Boz*, 1836–7, *Tales: The Boarding House*.
23   *Notes & Queries*, 1st Series, vol. 1, p. 414, quoted in T.S. Crawford, op. cit. p. 114.
24   T.S. Crawford, op. cit. p. 116.
25   The *Penny Magazine*, vol. V, No. 241, 2 January 1836.
26   The Marquis Caraccioli, *Picturesque and Sententious Dictionary*, quoted in T.S. Crawford, op. cit. p. 118.
27   *The Letters of Horace Walpole*, ed. Mrs Paget Toynbee, Clarendon Press, 1904, vol. 6, p. 309, quoted in T.S. Crawford, op. cit. p. 116.
28   M. Dorothy George, *Hogarth to Cruikshank, Social Change in Graphic Satire*, Penguin, 1967, figs. 137, 138.
29   P.J. Grosley, *A Tour to London*, 1772, vol. 1, p. 45, quoted in T.S. Crawford, op. cit. p. 116.
30   John Macdonald, *Memoirs of an Eighteenth Century Footman*, London 1790, quoted in T.S. Crawford, op. cit. p. 124.
31   Sir W.R. Drake, *Heathiana*, London 1881, p. 21, quoted in T.S. Crawford, op. cit. pp. 117-18.
32   T.S. Crawford, op. cit. pp. 119-20.
33   The Revd G.C. Renouard, to *Notes & Queries*, quoted in W. Sangster, op. cit. p. 48.
34   Loc. cit. p. 49.
35   W. Sangster, op. cit. p. 45.
36   *Report of the Juries . . .* , p. 657.
37   C.W. & P. Cunnington, *A Handbook of English Costume in the 19th Century*, Faber & Faber, 1959, p. 97.
38   Dr Cleland, *A Statistical Account of Glasgow*, quoted in the *Penny Magazine*, op. cit.
39   Verity Anderson, *The Northrepps Grandchildren*, Hodder & Stoughton, 1968.
40   Captain Gronow, *Reminiscences*, quoted in Pearl Binder, *The Peacock's Tail*, Harrap, 1958.
41   Jane Austen, *Persuasion*, published posthumously 1818, ch. 13.
42   Ibid. ch. 19.
43   Captain Jesse, *The Life of George Brummell Esq, commonly called Beau Brummell*, J.C. Nimmo. 1886, vol. II, p. 70.
44   Charles Dickens, *Martin Chuzzlewit*, 1843–4, chapters 19 and 49.

CHAPTER 4
1   *World of Fashion*, 1838, quoted in Anne Buck, *Victorian Costume & Costume Accessories*, Herbert Jenkins, 1961, p. 179.
2   Cf. S. Levitt, 'Registered Designs: New Source Material for the Study of the mid-Nineteenth Century Fashion Industry', in *Costume*, the Journal of the Costume Society, number 15, 1981, p. 49.
3   Most of the information about W. & J. Sangster's parasols is taken from advertisements in the *Illustrated London News*.
4   Advertisement in the *Illustrated London News*, 22 March 1851, p. 245.
5   Advertisement in the *Illustrated London News*, 18 April 1846.
6   Advertisement for Bailey & Co., St Paul's Churchyard, selling the bankrupt stock of D.K. Price & Son, 6 Pilgrim Street, Ludgate Hill, London. *Illustrated London News*, 6 May 1843, p. 313.
7   *Illustrated London News*, 13 August 1842.
8   The *Lady's Newspaper*, quoted in Anne Buck, op. cit. pp. 180-81.
9   Advertisement for John Morland & Son, 50 Eastcheap, London Bridge, *Illustrated London News*, 2 February 1850, p. 79.

10 Advertisement in the *Illustrated London News*, 1 May 1852, p. 359.

11 For example, in *Le Follet*, 1852, Victoria & Albert Museum, E2483-1888.

12 Advertisement in the *Illustrated London News*, 13 April 1850, p. 255.

13 The *Englishwoman's Domestic Magazine*, New Series, vol. 5, July 1862, p. 142.

14 Ibid. vol. 7, June 1863, p. 95.

15 Ibid. vol. 5, July 1862, p. 142.

16 Ibid. vol. 5, June 1862, p. 93.

17 Ibid. vol. 7, June 1863, p. 95.

18 Advertisement in the *Illustrated London News*, 12 January 1850.

19 *Punch*, quoted in C.W. & P. Cunnington, *A Handbook of English Costume in the 19th Century*, Faber & Faber, 1959, p. 226.

20 *International Exhibition Official Catalogue*, 1862, vol. II, No. 4814.

21 The *Milliner, Dressmaker & Warehouseman's Gazette*, June 1874, pp. 12–13.

CHAPTER 5

1 *Cassell's Family Magazine*, 1879, p. 373.

2 Ibid., August 1880, p. 571.

3 Ibid.

4 *Cassell's Family Magazine*, May 1880, p. 378.

5 Ibid., October 1880, p. 696.

6 The *Girl's Own Paper*, vol. X, No. 504, 24 August 1889, p. 748.

7 Ibid., vol. II, No. 82, 23 July 1881, p. 680.

8 Ibid., vol. IV, No. 186, 21 July 1883, p. 661.

9 Ibid.

10 Ibid.

11 Octave Uzanne, *The Sunshade, the Glove, the Muff*, J.C. Nimmo & Bain, 1883, pp. 63-4.

12 The *Girl's Own Paper*, vol. II, No. 82, 23 July 1881, p. 680.

13 The *Queen*, 5 April 1879, p. 290.

14 The *Girl's Own Paper*, vol. III, No. 126, 27 May 1882, p. 554.

15 Ibid., vol. V, No. 235, 28 June 1884, p. 618.

16 Ibid., vol. VI, No. 283, 30 May 1885, p. 353.

17 The *Woman at Home*, vol. IV, June 1895, p. 234.

18 *Cassell's Family Magazine*, May 1888, p. 378.

19 The *Girl's Own Paper*, vol. III, No. 142, 16 September 1882, p. 815.

20 Ibid., vol. IV, no. 174, 28 April 1883, p. 474.

21 Ibid., vol. V, No. 239, 26 July 1884, p. 682.

22 The *Lady's Pictorial*, 17 March 1888, p. 272.

23 *Cassell's Family Magazine*, April 1888, p. 312.

24 The *Girl's Own Paper*, vol. VI, 29 August 1885, p. 762.

25 The *Lady's World*, 1887, quoted in Anne Buck, *Victorian Costume & Costume Accessories*, Herbert Jenkins, 1961, p. 182.

26 *Cassell's Family Magazine*, May 1894, p. 474.

27 Ibid.

28 The *Woman at Home*, vol. V, June 1896, p. 793.

29 Ibid., vol. V, September 1896, p. 1028.

30 The *Lady's Realm*, vol. V, April 1899, p. 734.

31 Ibid., vol. 18, May 1905, p. 118.

32 Ibid., vol. VI, June 1899, p. 234.

33 The *Bag, Portmanteau & Umbrella Trader*, 17 May 1911.

34 The *Ladies' Field*, 6 April 1912, p. 252.

35 The *Bag, Portmanteau & Umbrella Trader*, 25 January 1911.

36 Ibid.

37 Ibid., April 1908.

38 The *Ladies' Field*, 6 April 1912, p. 252.

39 The *Bag, Portmanteau & Umbrella Trader*, May 1908.

40 Ibid., 21 September 1910.

41 Ibid., August 1907, illustrated November 1907.

42 The *Tailor & Cutter*, 1 August 1894, p. 240.

43 The *Bag, Portmanteau & Umbrella Trader*, July and October 1907.

44 The *Girl's Own Paper*, vol. V, No. 204, 24 November 1883, p. 122.

45 Ibid., vol. V, No. 231, 31 May 1884, p. 554.

46 The *Lady's Pictorial*, 3 December 1887, p. 565.

47 The *Woman at Home*, vol. III, February 1895, p. 469.

48 Ibid., December 1898, p. 333.

49 The *Bag, Portmanteau & Umbrella Trader*, March 1909.

50 British Patent, 15,080 of 1894.

51 The *Bag, Portmanteau & Umbrella Trader*, March 1908.

52 Ibid., 14 September 1910.

53 The Revd Francis Kilvert, *Diary*, entry for Friday, 28 April 1876.

54 *Cassell's Family Magazine*, 1879, p. 373.

55 The *Girl's Own Paper*, vol. X, No. 491, 25 May 1889, p. 537.

56 Reference to parasols at James Smith & Sons, New Oxford Street, London, in the *Bag, Portmanteau & Umbrella Trader*, August 1907.

57 The *Bag, Portmanteau & Umbrella Trader*, March 1908.

58 Design number 549864, registered about 24 September 1909; other numbers on Piccolo umbrellas usually refer to the designs of the handles.

59 A. Varron, *Paper Umbrellas in China and Japan*,

Ciba Review 1942, No. 142, p. 1541.

60   A. Adburgham, *Liberty's: A Biography of a Shop*, Allen & Unwin, 1975, p. 22.

CHAPTER 6

1   The *Bag, Portmanteau & Umbrella Trader*, May 1919, p. 14.
2   N. Hartnell, *Silver and Gold*, Evans, London 1955, p. 97.
3   *Woman's Journal*, August 1967.
4   *Vogue*, June 1974.
5   Quoted in the *Bag, Portmanteau & Umbrella Trader*, July 1919.
6   J. Amherst, *Wandering Abroad*, Secker & Warburg, 1976, p. 58.
7   For instance in *Housewife*, December 1962.
8   The *Sketch*, 5 February 1919.
9   The *Gentlewoman*, 21 March 1925, p. 336.
10   Ibid.
11   John Barker & Co., London, 1938 catalogue.
12   S. Moxon, *A Fox Centenary, Umbrella Frames 1848–1948*, S. Fox & Co., n.d.
13   Information from the Textile Institute, Manchester, and Mr Peter Lennox Kerr.
14   T. S. Crawford, *A History of the Umbrella*, David & Charles, 1970, p. 198.

Glossary

A disposition   1850s; used to describe dresses in which the flounces and often the bodice trimmings are woven or printed to match one another.

Alpaca   a fabric with cotton warps, the wefts of the wool of the South American llama; in 1848 W. Sangster was granted patent No. 12,056 for the use of this material as covering for parasols and umbrellas.

Antler   the horn of various species of deer, that of the Red Deer being the most frequently used, commonly found as handles of walking sticks and hunting whips, more seldom on umbrellas; often mistakenly called 'bone'.

Bakelite   a plastic, urea-formaldehyde resin, patented in about 1907 by Leo Baekeland (1863–1944).

Beadweaving   the method of incorporating beads into fabric during the weaving by using one set of warps and two sets of wefts.

Bedfordshire Maltese lace   bobbin-made lace in black silk or cream cotton, initially copied from the genuine Maltese lace shown at the Great Exhibition in 1851.

Bramble   the branches and roots of the wild rose and the blackberry, used for umbrella and parasol handles.

Brocaded   a weaving technique with the pattern usually in different colours from the background, done with the pattern threads taken in for each individual motif.

Broderie anglaise   a type of embroidery in white thread on white fabric, the pattern composed chiefly of holes.

Brussels lace   fine bobbin or needle-made lace produced in and around Brussels in Belgium; the lace found on parasols is *point de gaze*, a very high-quality needle lace, 'appliqué' bobbin lace, sometimes with needle-made details, sewn on to machine-made net, and 'duchesse de Bruxelles', a bobbin lace with insertions of *point de gaze*.

Calico   in the seventeenth century a fine cotton fabric akin to present-day lawn, rather than the coarse cotton cloth to which this name is now given; originally from Calicut in India.

Carrickmacross lace   of two types, one with the pattern in cut muslin applied to machine-made net, the other a guipure with the muslin linked by needleworked bars, taking its name from Carrickmacross in Ireland.

Celluloid   a plastic made by combining nitrated cellulose and camphor, discovered in 1883, also known as xylonite.

Chatelaine   article worn by women at the waist, and fashionable at various times between 1740 and 1890; basically a belt hook with a number of chains on which needlework tools, watches, fans and so forth were suspended; made in gold, silver, steel and other metals.

Chiffon   a semi-transparent silk muslin.

Chiné   any fabric in which the warp threads are printed before weaving, thus giving a blurred appearance to the pattern.

Chrysoprase   an apple-green variety of chalcedony; a crystalline quartz.

Cluny lace a bobbin-made coarse cotton lace with bold pattern; from the 1860s onwards.

Cockade fan a fan opening to a complete circle, the elongated guard sticks forming the handle.

Congo the name given to the wood of both the sweet- and horse-chestnut trees, when used for walking sticks and umbrella handles.

Coral a marine gem composed largely of calcium carbonate and produced by the coral polyp; there are many types of coral and the one favoured as parasol handles is the strong vermilion-coloured *Corallium rubrum*.

Cornelian a semi-precious stone; a semi-transparent, orange-red-coloured variety of quartz.

Crêpe de Chine a thin silk fabric with twisted wefts, having a crinkly surface.

Crêpe lisse a very thin crepe-like gauze chiefly used for frills, ruffles and widows' indoor caps.

Cretonne an unglazed twilled cotton fabric, colour-printed, usually with floral patterns.

Crochet a type of lace made with a single thread in a variety of knots and loops by means of a hooked needle; much was amateur made, although Irish crochet was professionally produced.

Crocidolite semi-precious stone, a variety of quartz, often called 'cat's eye' and 'tiger's eye'.

Crystal either the natural rock-crystal which is a colourless transparent variety of quartz, or fine-quality lead glass, which is also commonly called 'crystal'.

Directoire a style of women's costume fashionable in the 1870s and revived between 1907 and 1912, which borrowed details of men's clothes of the French Directory period of 1795–9; with regard to parasols Directoire refers to particularly long sticks.

En-tout-cas a cross between an umbrella and a parasol which could be used equally well in rainy or sunny weather. It was often more brightly coloured than an umbrella and plainer than a parasol, being without external trimming.

Erinoid a plastic made from powdered milk and so named because the milk came from Ireland; introduced in about 1897.

Foulard a soft thin-twilled washing silk.

Georgette a thin sheer crêped fabric, of silk or imitations.

Gingham (from the Malay *gingang*) a striped (or more recently, a checked) cotton, cotton and silk, or cotton and linen cloth in use in England since the seventeenth century. On umbrellas it was usually of cotton, with a band of raised or multi-coloured stripes near the edge of the cover. The French for gingham, *guingamp*, is also the name of a town in Brittany.

Glacé a thin plain-weave silk fabric with a lustrous surface.

Gloria a silk and wool mixture fabric, as far as is known used only for umbrella covers; *silésienne* is the French name for this material.

Gros de Naples a silk fabric with a corded shiny surface.

Grosgrain a corded silk fabric, thicker than *gros de Naples*.

Guipure lace in which the motifs are linked by bars rather than by net; Irish guipure could be either Carrickmacross lace or fine crochet.

Holly branches of the common holly (*Ilex aquifolium*) used for driving whips, walking sticks and umbrella handles, and always left with the natural knots proud.

Honiton lace made in and around Honiton in Devon, the bobbin lace from this area is similar to Brussels, and lace with bobbin-made motifs applied on to net is the type usually found on parasol covers.

Horn various types of horn from cattle was used, particularly that of African and Indian buffalo which is known as Cape horn.

Jaconet a thin plain-weave cotton fabric, thicker than muslin.

76 Key to component parts and shapes of cover and handle.

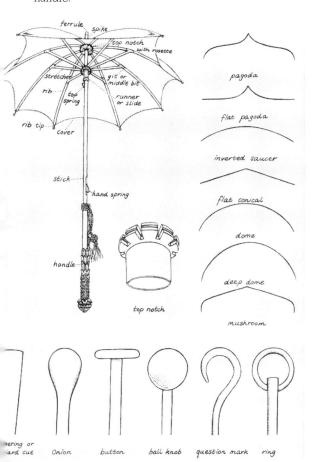

Japanned in the seventeenth and early eighteenth centuries this meant imitation Oriental lacquer, but was later used for merely painted wood or metal.

Jet in the context of parasol trimmings, probably 'French jet' (black glass) was used, rather than the true jet, which is fossilized pine wood.

Lancewood a flexible wood from South America, used for umbrella sticks.

Lapis lazuli a semi-precious stone of a deep-blue colour, often with inclusions of iron pyrites – 'fools gold'. Much imitation lapis was made of glass.

Laventine a silk and very fine cotton mixture cloth, as far as it is known used only for umbrella covers.

Lawn a thin plain-weave fabric, originally of linen, later of cotton.

Leavers lace made on a net machine invented by John Leavers in Nottingham in 1813; from the 1830s close copies of handmade lace were produced on it.

Malacca a smooth type of bamboo native to Malaysia, prized for the beauty of its naturally mottled surface.

Maltese lace a black or cream silk bobbin-made lace, patterned with wheatear motifs and usually Maltese crosses.

Merveilleux a soft twilled satin.

Moiré a ribbed silk fabric with irregular 'watered' patterns.

Muslin a semi-transparent cotton fabric of plain, rather open weave.

Ombre fabric or yarn shaded from pale to dark in one colour.

Onyx semi-precious stone, a variety of quartz; various colours are found but black with white stripes is the most common.

Parkesine a plastic made from pyroxyline and oil by Alexander Parkes, of Birmingham; invented *c.* 1856 but in general production only after 1862.

Partridge cane a type of bamboo with slightly pronounced knots and of a dark brown colour with yellow streaks; thought to resemble the markings on a partridge's wings.

Pattens overshoes with wooden soles raised on iron rings to raise the wearer above wet and dirt when walking.

Pekin a silk fabric with stripes of contrasting texture.

Pimento wood of the Jamaica Pepper tree, an evergreen of the myrtle family, used for parasol handles.

Point lace an abbreviation for needlepoint lace, sometimes used for fine bobbin-made lace; in the second half of the nineteenth century the term could refer to a high-quality needlepoint lace such as Brussels *point de gaze*, or to lace made from hand- or machine-made tape connected together by needlework.

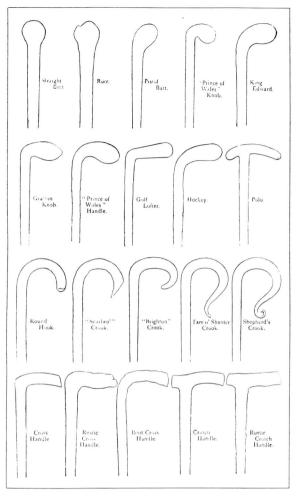

77 Outlines of shapes of stick handles, from a journal of 1910.

Pompadour small floral patterns, often pink or blue, fashionable in the 1870s.

Poult de soie Chinée a corded silk fabric, presumably with a *chiné* pattern.

Pusher lace lace made on the Pusher machine which was invented by James Clarke in 1813; much was produced in imitation of black Chantilly lace.

PVC polyvinyl chloride, a plastic derived from oil or natural gas.

Raffia a fibre obtained from the Madagascar raphia palm, and much used, both in the natural colour and dyed, for embroidery in the 1920s.

Ridicule otherwise 'reticule', a lady's handbag, usually of small size, early nineteenth century.

Serge a twilled worsted cloth.

Shantung a thin plain-weave fabric of undyed silk.

Silésienne see *gloria*.

Spanish lace   a hand- or machine-made black or cream silk lace with bold, dense patterns.

Spitalfields   in the context of umbrellas, a silk fabric used for covers.

Surah   a soft shiny twilled Indian silk fabric, thicker than foulard.

Taffeta   as a covering for umbrellas, a silk-and-cotton mixture fabric.

Tatting   a type of lace made with either one or two threads in a variety of knots and rings by means of one or sometimes two small shuttles. Much was amateur-made, although Irish tatting was professionally produced.

Thistlewood   a lightweight wood, apparently some kind of bramble, with pronounced knots, used for parasol handles in the 1880s.

Thorn   the wood of the common blackthorn (*Prunus spinosa*), and much used for driving whips, walking sticks and umbrella handles, with the natural knots left proud.

Tortoiseshell   not a true shell, but the carapace of the Hawksbill and Loggerhead turtles. Varying in colour from dark brown to pale yellow with contrasting mottled patterns, it can also be dyed, and was much imitated in horn and various plastics.

Tulle   a fine silk machine-made net.

Tussore   a plain-weave fabric of natural brownish-coloured silk which is produced by the Tussah moth of Burma.

Whalebone   not true bone, but a horn-like substance in sheet form replacing teeth in the Mystacoceti whale, and cut into strips which were laminated together for umbrella and parasol ribs.

Whangee   a type of bamboo, of a pale-yellow colour with pronounced knots, also found with a blackened surface produced by scorching.

Xylonite   see *celluloid*.

Zanella   a sateen-like fabric with cotton warp and wool weft, as far as is known used only for umbrella covers.

Museums to Visit

The museums that were visited while carrying out research for this book are listed in the Acknowledgment. The largest collections are in:

The Gallery of English Costume, Platt Hall, Rusholme, Manchester

The Museum of Costume, the Assembly Rooms, Bath

The Museum of London, London Wall, London EC2

The Victoria & Albert Museum, South Kensington, London

The Welsh Folk Museum, St Fagan's, Cardiff

but even the smaller collections, such as those in Cheltenham and Derby, yielded unexpected treasures. Most museums that have costume collections will have some parasols and a few umbrellas, but little, if anything, will be actually on display. It would be worth while to enquire at your local museum, or consult the list of costume museums in *A Handbook of Costume* by Janet Arnold (Macmillan, 1973).

Select Bibliography

Adburgham, A., *A Punch History of Manners and Modes, 1841–1941*, Hutchinson 1961.
    Shops and Shopping, Allen & Unwin, 1964.

Arnold, J., *A Handbook of Costume*, Macmillan 1973.

Blum, S., *Ackermann's Costume Plates 1818–1828*, Dover.
    Victorian Fashions and Costumes from Harper's Bazaar, 1867–98, Dover, 1974.

Booth, C., *Life and Labour of the People in London*, London 1889.

Bradfield, N., *Costume in Detail*, Harrap, 1968.

Buck, A., *Dress in Eighteenth Century England*, Batsford, 1979.
    Victorian Costume and Costume Accessories, Herbert Jenkins, 1961.

Byrde, P., *The Male Image: Men's Fashion in England, 1300–1970*, Batsford, 1979.

Crawford, T.S., *A History of the Umbrella*, David & Charles, 1970.

Cunnington, C.W. *English Women's Clothing in the Nineteenth Century*, Faber, 1937.
    English Women's Clothing in the Present Century, Faber, 1952.

Cunnington, C.W. & P., *A Handbook of English Costume in the Eighteenth Century*, Faber, 1957.
    A Handbook of English Costume in the Nineteenth Century, Faber, 1959, 1970.

D'Allemagne, H.R., *Les Accessoires du Costume*, 3 Vols. Schemit, 1928.

Diderot, D., *L'Encyclopédie, ou Dictionnaire Raisonné des Sciences, des Arts et des Métiers*, 1751.
    Encyclopédie Méthodique, volume 5 of *Arts et Métiers Mécaniques*, Paris, 1783.

Foster, V., *A Visual History of Costume, the Nineteenth Century*, Batsford, 1984.

Gaunt, W., *The Great Century of British Painting: Hogarth to Turner*, Phaidon Press, 1971.

George, M.D., *Hogarth to Cruikshank, Social Change in Graphic Satire*, Penguin, 1967.

Girtin, T., *Makers of Distinction*, Harvill Press, London, 1959.

Hébert, L., *The Engineer's and Mechanic's Encyclopaedia*, London 1836.

Hughes, T., *Small Antiques for the Collector*, Lutterworth Press, 1964.

Lester, K.M. & Oerke, B.V., *Accessories of Dress*, C.A. Bennett, Peora, USA 1940.

Mansfield, A. & Cunnington, P., *A Handbook of English Costume in the Twentieth Century*, Faber, 1973.

Moxon, S., *A Fox Centenary, Umbrella Frames, 1848–1948*, S. Fox & Co. n.d. (*c.* 1949).

Sangster, W., *Umbrellas and their History*, Cassell, Pelter & Galpin, n.d. (*c.* 1870).

Timmins, S., *The Resources, Products and Industrial History of Birmingham*, London 1866.

Uzanne, O., *The Sunshade, the Glove and the Muff*, Nimmo & Bain, London, 1883.

Varron, A., *The History of the Umbrella and the Sunshade*, Ciba Review, No. 142, 1942.

von Boehn, M., *Modes and Manners: the Eighteenth Century*, Dent, 1929.
    Modes and Manners: Ornaments, Dent, 1929.

Wood, C., *Victorian Panorama*, Faber, 1976.

Index

The numbers in italics denote those *pages* on which illustrations occur. 'Pl.' refers to the colour plates.